KING OF THE ROAD

TRUE TALES FROM A LEGENDARY ICE ROAD TRUCKER

ALEX DEBOGORSKI

WILEY

John Wiley & Sons, Inc.

To my dear wife, Louise, for putting up with my shenanigans in
the past and future.

To all my children, grandchildren, and onward: I do expect each one of you to put
more into life than you take out.

To all those who have made the world a better place but no one has ever heard of,
including Charlie Eddy, Ernie Running Bear, and Francis "Fats" Newton.

Published by John Wiley & Sons, Inc., Hoboken, New Jersey.

Design by Forty-five Degree Design LLC

The views and opinions expressed in this book are those of the author and do not necessarily reflect the views and opinions of A&E Television Networks, LLC or HISTORY®.

For general information about our other products and services, please contact our Customer Care Department within the United States at (800) 762-2974, outside the United States at (317) 572-3993 or fax (317) 572-4002.

Wiley also publishes its books in a variety of electronic formats. Some content that appears in print may not be available in electronic books. For more information about Wiley products, visit our web site at www.wiley.com.

Library of Congress Cataloging-in-Publication Data:

Debogorski, Alex, date.
  King of the road : true tales from a legendary ice road trucker / Alex Debogorski.
    p. cm.
  Includes bibliographical references and index.
  ISBN 978-0-470-64368-6 (hardback); ISBN 978-0-470-92879-0 (ebk);
  ISBN 978-0-470-92880-6 (ebk); ISBN 978-0-470-92881-3 (ebk)
  1. Debogorski, Alex, 1953– 2. Truck drivers–Canada–Anecdotes. 3. Ice crossings–Alaska–Anecdotes. 4. Ice crossings–Canada–Anecdotes. 5. Trucking–Anecdotes.
6. Ice road truckers (Television program) I. Title.
  HD8039.M7952C364 2010
  388.3′24092–dc22

                                          2010033497

Printed in the United States of America

10 9 8 7 6 5 4 3 2

CONTENTS

ACKNOWLEDGMENTS

My acknowledgments first go to God, who with infinite wisdom knew me before the firmament and according to His plan put me in the Peace River country of Alberta, Canada, on August 4, 1953. I especially appreciate His patience and pray that I may continue my earthly trip, loaded or empty, sometimes receiving pay and sometimes making my donation.

I must salute all those of the Northwest Territories of Canada, where I make my home. Really, they are responsible for most of my character and humor. Having laughed at my jokes, breathed the same air, and given me heck as often as not over thirty-five years, my northern people have helped make me who I am.

All those who I worked with, traveled with, and sometimes only ran into, impacted me—and I them—not always in a positive fashion. It's been a slice.

Thanks to Jake MacDonald, the writer who helped me turn these stories into a finished book.

Thanks to my literary agent, Rick Broadhead, for helping to make this book happen and for introducing me to my publishers.

PROLOGUE

I'm six-three, 250 pounds.

Fifty-seven years old. Busted up from one end to the other. Too many accidents to recall, and plenty of fights. Some of which I won, but some of which I lost, and I mean *lost*. Lost them bad enough to end up on crutches. I've been hit by a train and run over by a truck the size of a house. Broke my nose eight times. Been stabbed and burned and almost frozen to death. If I took off my clothes and stood in front of a doctor, he might laugh. "Well, Mr. Debogorski, you're quite a sight. You look like a big old dump truck—beat up and battered all over, with some creaky joints and a lot of miles on the odometer—but I still wouldn't want to get in your way."

When you get to my age, you start realizing that you've got more road in your rearview mirror than ahead of you. I've got a big family, a tribe of grandkids, and more bills than a man could pay by working around the clock. So I've got lots to think about. Sometimes, late at night, I'll lie there in the dark with my eyes wide open. That's when I try to think of something peaceful.

I've got a memory where I'm about three or four years old, maybe younger. It's a warm summer afternoon and I'm lying in my crib. We are living in a little log cabin out in the woods and the crib is right beneath an open window. I'm looking up into the branches of a big poplar tree, and the leaves are rustling and the warm summer wind is coming in through the screen. My mother is in the kitchen baking, and the house is full of the nice smell of fresh bread. I'm supposed to be napping, but I'm too happy to go to sleep. I've got clean sheets in my crib and I'm looking up at those silvery leaves rustling in the wind and the whole world is right.

When I got a little older life got more complicated. We were poor, but we were clothed and fed, so it wasn't like we were hurting for the basic necessities of life. But the kids at school made fun of me because of where I grew up. People who spend a lot of time alone out in nature tend to be different from others. They think their own thoughts and they come up with their own ideas about things. I learned how to imitate all the different birds and animals, and they were my main friends. I could make bird calls and yip like a coyote. The kids thought I was pretty comical. But most of the time they weren't laughing *with* me, they were laughing *at* me.

They also made fun of me because I was big. You wouldn't think that being big would be a handicap in school, but I was clumsy. I was always running around tripping over things. When we took phys ed class in school all the other kids had proper running shoes, but I just had the felt liners of boots. As you can imagine, the gym floor was slippery, and I was always skidding into kids and knocking them over. One poor kid would be crawling around like he'd been hit by a truck and the other kids would be laughing like hell. I didn't exactly wear fashionable clothes, either. My parents were recent immigrants, and they gave us clothes that were meant to keep you warm and dry—not to make you look good. And you were expected to wear those same clothes for years! I had one fur hat that was so old it was turning orange. So you can imagine how the kids had fun commenting on my unfashionable appearance.

I was good-natured, so it was safe to make fun of me. But kids can be mean and vicious. One time we were going out into the yard for recess and as soon as I came out the door this kid spat in my face. I tried to catch him, but he was too fast. Every time I walked up to another kid, he would spit in my face. They were all too fast to catch, and by the end of recess I was just seething with frustration. I hadn't done anything, so I guess they were just tormenting me. Kids will get some mean idea and then right away they just do it.

Because we were raised in Canada, I joined the Canadian Air Cadets when I was a young teenager and won a bush survival course. Having grown up in the bush, I already had a jump on the other guys, and I did pretty well. I could use an ax and I could build a fire and I could skin a muskrat just like that. They only chose three kids from each province, and I got the best marks they'd seen in ten years, so that encouraged me. One time we went survival camping, and I was sitting on the bank of the Smoky River on the night that Neil Armstrong walked on the moon. I was looking up at the sky, looking at that big full moon, thinking of those spacemen up there and wondering if I was ever going to make something of myself.

1

EARLY DAYS

*"Born in a cave—what a way to improve
a resume."*

I guess that kid that I used to be would be surprised if he could see me now, forty years later, driving a huge Kenworth truck through the early darkness of a February morning. It's minus 42 degrees outside, and a hell of a lot nastier if you count the wind chill and the blowing snow. That kid would probably be a lot more surprised if I told him we're driving over water—deep water.

We've got almost three hundred feet of water under our tires, and if the ice fractures it will probably "hinge"—swing open like a trapdoor and then swing back shut after us, leaving no more sign of what happened than a set of tire tracks. Then we'd sink like a crowbar to the bottom. It would be so dark and spooky down at the bottom of this lake that I don't want to think about what would happen to us after we settled—probably upside-down, the windows smashed and maybe our heads caved in from the water pressure, the little creepy-crawlies and ice worms nosing into the cab to see if we're good to eat.

I know it's a little hard to believe we're on a lake, so I would roll down the window and tell him to have a listen—did you hear that sound a minute ago? That muffled sound like a rifle shot? That's the ice cracking under the weight of the truck. It doesn't mean the ice is going to give way. It's actually a good sound—it means we've got good ice beneath us, stiff thick ice that creaks when the weight of the truck crosses it. When it cracks it refreezes, and it's stronger than before. At least, that's what the road engineers tell us, and they're supposed to know what they're doing. They tell us bad ice is soft and flexible and doesn't make a sound if it's getting ready to fail. But other guys say the opposite. Some of the experienced old road builders argue that brittle ice breaks easier, and that cold weather is a dangerous time to be ice-road trucking. In my experience, ice gets stiffer as it gets colder. All ice is flexible, and it sags when you drive a truck across it. But it definitely gets more rigid in cold weather, and that can be a good thing or a bad thing, depending on how thick it is.

I could tell him all those things, but I don't want to scare the little guy.

Heck, I don't want to scare myself, either. There are trucks ahead of us and trucks behind us. The trucks usually travel in groups of four, spread a third of a mile apart. You keep separated because you don't want to put too much weight on one piece of ice road at the same time, but we keep in touch by radio, and if one guy has a serious problem he can usually rely on the other truckers to help him. Nighttime is the easiest time on the ice road. You can see the shadows, and it's less of a strain on your eyes. The highway patrol's at home having a beer, so you don't have to worry about them bothering you. Radio reception is good, and you can tune up the satellite radio and get caught up on world news. I like to spend an intensive period of time listening to politics from around the world. After I come off the ice road I don't have to read a newspaper for a couple of months because it takes that long for the fundamental changes to happen.

Nighttime is also the time when the truckers get talkative. It's lonely out here. Guys get on the radio and start telling each other stories. They're like little kids in a bunkhouse after the adults have put out the lights. Everybody is keeping each other company. I'm one of the most devoted storytellers on the ice road, and I'll keep the other truckers entertained for hours. I used to think that I should write down my life story one day—because I've had so many scrapes and almost been killed so many times that I can't believe I'm still here. I'm sure the other truckers would enjoy hearing about some of my hair-raising adventures. And all the good times, too. There are so many stories that I hardly know where to begin. But I guess the best way is to just imagine that it's nighttime and we're rolling along on the ice road. The headlights are poking through the darkness. The heater is purring away. I've got a hot cup of coffee in my hand, and I'm going to start where all stories start—at the beginning.

Escape from the Nazis

Let me tell you how lucky I am just to be here.

My parents and grandparents came from Poland, a beautiful country, with rolling hills and lots of good agricultural land, with such natural riches that for countless centuries, all kinds of warlords and aggressive nations fought over it like wolves fighting over a bone. When you think about what my family went through it's unbelievable that we survived.

In 1939, Nazi Germany and the Soviet Union signed a secret agreement that they would invade Poland and split it up between themselves. But they were lying to each other. Russia had no intention of giving Poland to the Germans and vice versa. Throughout the war, the Polish people were savaged by both invading nations. The Russians told the Poles they would back them up if they formed an underground army and fought against the Germans. It was a trick. When the Polish underground fought it out with the Germans in Warsaw, the Russians stood by with their arms folded and watched their two enemies bleed each other—figuring that it was making their own lives easier with each guy that was killed. Finally, the Germans slaughtered the Polish resistance fighters and set about destroying Warsaw. As punishment for the uprising, Hitler said, "Don't leave a single brick standing."

The death toll was incredible. Every day was like a World Trade Center attack, only it went on month after month. Millions of people died. Meanwhile, the Russians wanted their own piece of Poland for themselves, and the best way to control any country is to get rid of its capable people. As I understand it, in April 1940 the Russians rounded up 22,000 military officers, teachers, journalists, police officers, and other people of influence and executed them in a secret facility in the Katyn Forest. Each guy got one bullet in the back of the head. They'd throw the body on a truck and do the next guy. It was an assembly line, with an execution every three minutes. They would do this all night long, night after night. That's how they murdered 22,000 of the smartest people in Poland. In my opinion they probably did it because they figured it was the only way their country would be dumb enough to fall for communism.

My family on my mother's side was in the Polish underground, fighting the Nazis. My mother was beautiful. Blue-green eyes, six feet tall, and a swimmer and runner. All the women in my family were beautiful—tall and strong, long legs, and stacked. They looked like movie stars.

Sometimes there would be a knock on the door and it would be a little six-year-old kid bringing a message from the underground. For some reason, not even the Nazis suspected little kids that age. The kid would say, "The Gestapo is coming!"

Minutes later the Gestapo would pound on the door, looking for Jews or weapons or whatever incriminating evidence they could find. My family was always in danger because they often kept contraband in the house. I remember my mother telling me about the time the Nazis came and the piano was stuffed with hand grenades, so she and her sister, Auntie Lala (her nickname meant "doll" because she was so cute), sat down to play marching songs to distract them.

Imagine two beautiful teenage girls playing a piano full of high explosives. The Gestapo officers came in and listened and gave the women a pinch and then they left. My mother said they cried for twenty minutes afterward. They were just girls, and the whole time they were playing they had to keep calm because they thought that the German marching music played at top volume would set off the hand grenades and blow them all to smithereens. Another time they were hiding a Jewish man in the house and the Gestapo came. The Jewish fugitive was in the fold-down couch, and everybody sat on him while the Gestapo searched the house.

My dad and his family were shipped by the Bolsheviks to Siberia. At that time he was a teenager on the family farm in

Poland. After Stalin turned on his partner Hitler and joined the Allied war effort, one hundred thousand political prisoners were released from the Siberian gulags as a sign of good faith. Grandpa and Grandma Debogorski and three boys, minus two children who had died from starvation and disease in the gulag, made their way from Tehran, Iran, to Tanganyika, Africa, which is now Tanzania. There the British took those willing and able to fight. Grandpa went to the Africa campaign, and Dad went to Glasgow, Scotland, where he trained as a paratrooper. He jumped into Arnhem and Nijmegen in Holland as part of Operation Market Garden, made famous by the movie *A Bridge Too Far*.

My mother's father was a high-ranking military man. He was friends with some of the biggest statesmen in Europe at the time, especially in Eastern Europe, but they finally caught him smuggling Jews and his connections didn't help him. The Nazis sent him to Auschwitz and shot him with a firing squad. They told him they didn't want to put him in the oven and make him into soap because the soap would smell like garlic.

My grandmother, by then a widow, married a German officer. I never did get an explanation for that. They moved to Germany, and my mother went to work for a German SS lieutenant as a secretary. Mum told me she carried a briefcase with a handgun in the false bottom and continued with the work of the underground, smuggling Jews out of Germany. It's part of our history and I'd like to know more about it. I've been so busy all my life, working at one job or another, that I haven't been able to go back to the old country and research my family's history the way it deserves. After the war Mum moved to England, where she studied music and math at Cambridge University and met my dad in London.

Dad asked her to marry him, and they became Stanley and Irene Debogorski. In 1953 my parents moved to the Canadian province of Alberta, up in the Peace River country. It's a beautiful area of the world and actually looks a little bit like Poland, farmland interspersed with evergreen forest, with creeks and rivers and lots of wildlife. My grandparents on my father's side were already there, and my mum and dad set up a little farm across the road from them.

My mother devoted a lot of attention to me, her little Alex. She tried to teach me to play the piano and sing. If there was a party at Christmas or New Year's my mum would dress me up and I would sing and dance for the guests. I guess I was pretty comical, because everyone would laugh and clap like crazy. Then my mother would play the piano and we would sing together, those sad songs of the old country, my mother singing harmony in the background. Everyone tells me that I had a beautiful singing voice, although it's hard to believe that now!

Aunt Elsie

When Alex was young, I was married to his father's brother.

We would go and visit the grandparents on the farm, and Alex was always there, among the kids. I never really noticed him, to tell the truth. You know what kids are like. They run around in the yard. They're all more or less the same.

Then when he was nine years old he came and lived with me for two days. We were living in Peace River, in northern Alberta, and Alex's mom wanted to go into the recording studio and make some musical tapes. She was a striking woman, slim, six feet tall: and very good-looking. She came from a high-class family in the old country and she carried herself that way, very sophisticated and elegant. She was an accomplished musician and she wanted to go into the studio and record some tapes of her own music, so she showed up at my door with Alex and asked me to take care of him for two days. I was glad to take him. It's always fun to have kids in the house.

My impressions of him were quite different from the little ruffian that I used to see playing in the farmyard. He was quiet, very studious. A nice boy who was obviously very close to his mom. They were like two peas from the same pod. She told me that Alex was going to be a doctor or a lawyer or a politician. That was her plan for him. She was not going to let him grow up to be a farmer.

The whole time he stayed with me he had his nose in a book. He loved reading. He never gave me any trouble and had nice manners. He was tall for his age, like his mother, and even though he didn't do anything but read he was always hungry. I would put out a quart of milk and a bag of cookies so he could have a little snack and I'd come back five minutes later and the whole works would be gone. In the morning I would pour half a box of cereal into a salad bowl and he would gobble it down.

Years later, he still had that same appetite. The family came over one time for breakfast and I cooked a dozen eggs and a pound of bacon and put it on a platter on the table in front of Alex. I thought that everyone would take what they wanted, but Alex ate the whole platter, thinking that I'd made it for him.

Life on the farm was rough and tumble. But my mum was this polished, cultivated lady, so I grew up with two sides to my life.

I had the sensitive artistic side and the roughneck side. It was like I had two little genies sitting on my shoulders—one a poet and the other a wild man. They were both whispering in my ear, one urging me to be good, the other bad.

I was big, too, bigger than the other kids. I grew like a weed because of the diet they gave me when I was a baby. When I was only a few months old my mother started putting mashed potatoes and gravy into my milk bottle. By the time I was four years old I'd eat a whole salad bowl filled with porridge for breakfast, then top it off with some bacon and eggs. When I was finished with that I would run across the road to Grandma and Grandpa's and they'd give me another breakfast. She'd say, "Gosh, doesn't your mother feed you anything?" I was eating enough for two kids, and I was getting to be the size of two kids.

My mother always had high hopes for me. She thought I was the special one, the one who was going to be the doctor or lawyer. She wasn't always happy. Compared to the prewar aristocracy she left behind, all she had was poverty, dirt, hard work, and very little in the way of music and culture, all those fine things that she had grown up with. I think she suffered from post-traumatic stress from all the terrible things she saw during the war, and even though she was no longer in Poland or Germany, she carried all of those memories inside her, like ghosts.

She sometimes heard things and saw things that were strange. Maybe they were real. Maybe they weren't. It wasn't much help talking to the older people because they were even more superstitious than she was. That was the culture in the old country. Those East Europeans could go pick herbs in the bush and make medicine. The poor didn't have doctors. They relied on some old granny who was a medicine woman. In that sense they were more like Indians than white people. And they got along real well with the Indians, too. They had a lot in common. You might laugh at their beliefs, but if you spend any time with them they start making more sense.

When I was a kid I spent a lot of time with the Indians. There was a meadow next to our log house and native people from the Duncan reserve used to camp out in that field on their way up north to hunt moose. I visited with them and talked to them and learned to respect their culture, their values, and their way of thinking about the world. And in 1965, after my mum died, when I was twelve years old, a local native fellow named Ernie Runningbear helped take care of us in that awful transition time when we had no mother and Dad had to work all day. So I have a lot of admiration for Indians. They're humble people, have a healthy respect for the power of nature, and many of their ideas about medicines, spirits, and animals are similar to the ideas that my ancestors professed back in Poland.

Years later, I met a native guy in Yellowknife who had been cured of cancer by an Indian medicine man after doctors had given up on him. I was visiting him at his home in Northland Trailer Park. He boiled a pot of water on the stove, then grabbed a handful of vegetation and put it in the pot. He said he was making tea. I was shocked. I said, "My grandmother made tea with the same weeds." He told me that the medicine man from High Level, who was Cree, same as the native people from back in the Peace River country of Alberta, had told him to drink tea from these weeds and not drink alcohol. That way he would cure his cancer. That was over thirty years ago, and he's still alive today. When you live close to nature you learn about natural medicines, and the medicines seem to be the same cross-culturally.

So that was the local culture that my mother was raising her family in. It was like the old country in the sense that it was full of ghost stories and healers, but it was maybe a little on the bad side, because she had all these haunting memories from the war. Nowadays, medical people have a better understanding of how psychological trauma can injure a person. But we didn't have access to that kind of care. She was on her own, a long way from the home that was wiped out by war, surrounded by deep dark woods, and I know she got spooked at times.

One time she was at home by herself while we were at school and Dad was working on the railroad. This was about 1961, when I was eight years old. The cows got out of the corral. Someone had left the gate open and the cows all wandered off. We had about forty or fifty head at the time. She went outside and tried to start the old John Deere tractor but she couldn't get it going and she was very upset because she knew that Dad would be angry. Meanwhile, the cows were heading off down the road and out of sight. She went back into the house to have herself a good cry, and then she saw something out the window and there were the cows coming back!

They were being herded by an old man with a white beard and a big collie. The dog would run after the cows and make sure they were going into the gate, and went right back to the man and he would pat the dog like he was encouraging it. She told us the old man with the collie herded the cows until every last one was through the gate. Mum hurried back into the house and put the tea on and started preparing something to eat. She went outside to invite him in but he was gone. The gate was still open so she closed it and walked down the road looking for him. There was nobody there. She ended up walking all the way down to the corner—three-quarters of a mile—but he had disappeared. It had rained all summer and the road was pure mud, but there were no tracks in the ground, just the tracks of the cows.

She went and talked to her neighbor, Lloyd Newton, who lived a mile away, and Lloyd told her that the only thing he could think of was that there used to be a ghost up north of our place. He said he'd seen it several times up in the pasture. It was an old man with a collie and the dog would jump up to his shoulder. The best thing that Lloyd could figure was that this same ghost had brought the cows home. My mother was sure that she had been visited by a ghost.

She had all kinds of other fears. I remember her telling us once that the ground of Poland was soaked with blood because of all the wars the country had endured for centuries. She told us a story about a trip her mother made in Poland. They were in a stagecoach crossing a wide-open plain when they noticed a huge black ball rolling along behind them. The driver was frightened and whipped the horses, but no matter how fast they galloped this ball, about eight feet in diameter, was rolling right along beside them. She said it was the Devil's Ball. It was made up of all evil things. They finally got to the town and the ball disappeared, to their great relief.

When we were kids we were fascinated by this story of the Devil's Ball, and we used to beg her to tell us about other scary things that had happened in the old country. She would say, "No, I can't tell you. You're too young."

We never got to hear about most of them because she started having a lot of problems with depression, and when I was 12 years old, in 1965, she hanged herself. She was tough enough to survive the Nazis, but she couldn't stand the isolation of the backwoods and the gnawing memories of her past. My dad was left alone with five kids and little help. My siblings are Richard, Mark, Simone, and Gregory. Gregory, the youngest, was six months old and I, the oldest, was twelve. Social Services was going to take us away, but my dad fought them off and managed to keep me, my brothers Richard and Mark, and my sister Simone at home. My little brother Greg was considered too young and he ended up in foster care for three years.

It was very different once my mum was gone. I did most of the housework and looked after myself and three siblings. I cooked, cleaned, and washed the laundry. My dad was a hard taskmaster. He said, "I guess Mother wanted you to be a doctor, did she? Well, I agree, but you need more discipline."

He learned discipline from twelve years in the British military and would give out a licking at the drop of a hat. I don't know how many willow switches he broke across my rear end. At school one time I went to sit down and forgot that my ass was sore. As soon as my rear end touched the seat, I jumped up. The teacher said, "Alex, what's wrong? Did someone put a tack on your chair?"

I sat back down as gently as possible and I said, "No, ma'am, I'm fine."

I didn't want anyone to know that my dad had been whipping me.

Wild Animals Were My Friends

When I was growing up, nature amazed me, scared me, and sometimes tickled me on a daily basis. When I was three years old, it was the bear that was standing at the front door. I opened the door with my cap gun in my hand, and when I saw the bear only four feet away, I got off two shots before my mother grabbed me by the scruff of the neck and dragged me back into the house. It was the mouse that I found in my pocket when I was eight years old. It took me a minute to figure out what the tickling was, then I kind of jumped, and the mouse was as startled as I was.

It was the bird that used to nest every year under the eaves of our log house. It was the most beautiful shade of blue, like the sky. It was darker blue on top and lighter blue underneath, and it had the most beautiful song you've ever heard. It wasn't a Rocky Mountain bluebird and it wasn't like any other type of bird. That pretty little thing built a nest under our roof overhang every year until around the time that my mum died. Then it disappeared, and I never saw it again.

I remember one of my pets was a coyote. I was maybe twelve years old, walking home from school, and I spotted this coyote lying in the ditch. I don't know what was wrong with it, but it didn't look too healthy. I went home and got my little wagon and went back and picked up the coyote and loaded him into the wagon. I took him home, put a collar on him, and tied him up to a tree with a long rope. I fed him some scraps and gave him some milk and over the next few days he started to come around. The coyote and I got along pretty well. He was well behaved and made a good pet. I had lots of pets growing up, chickens, pigs, dogs, a steer, but this was my first coyote.

One day I came home from school and there was my coyote lying there with no head. I went and found Dad and said, "What happened to my coyote?"

He said, "The police killed it and took its head."

"Why did they do that?"

"It was foaming at the mouth, so they thought it might have rabies. So they cut off its head and sent it to the university."

What good is a pet coyote with no head? I was upset, but I got over it. There were animals everywhere and a potential pet behind every bush and under every stone. We had a team of Belgian horses to do the farm work, cutting hay and hauling grain, and while my dad was driving the team my little brother Richie and I were always trying to push each other off the wagon. My dad would wait until we were both rolling on the ground, then he'd speed up the horses and we had to run like heck to catch up with him. He'd keep the horses going just a bit faster than us.

So we were chasing the wagon across the field one day when my brother and I spotted a great horned owl that couldn't fly. It was young but it was an immense thing, about two feet high, so of course we wanted to keep it for a pet. My dad told us to let it go, but somehow we won the argument and took it home and made it into a pet. It was like having your own personal feathered kite. It had huge wings, about four feet across, and Richie and I would run across the yard and throw that owl in the air. It would glide for quite a ways and land on the ground. Then we'd pick it up and turn around and fly it the other way.

My dad didn't want us to have the owl because we had a nice flock of pigeons in the barn and he was convinced the owl would go after them. He kept saying, "That damn bird is going to eat all our pigeons."

We kept saying, "No, Dad, our owl won't eat pigeons."

For a week or ten days we played with that owl every day, running back and forth across the yard and flying him like a kite. Finally one day we tossed him in the air and he just kept going!

We called him but he wouldn't come back. We thought that was pretty ungrateful. Heck, we took care of him and then he just left!

A few days later, my dad noticed a few pigeon feathers lying on the ground beside the barn. Within a month there wasn't a pigeon left on the property.

Dad Buys a Wife

When my mum passed away, in 1965, I was twelve years old and I had four younger brothers and sisters, including my youngest brother, Greg. He was only six months old and had to go to a foster home for a while before my dad managed to get him back.

I didn't realize it at the time, but the government Social Services people were trying to take us away from Dad and put us in foster care. Dad was having a hard time looking after both us and the farm, so he was always looking for a woman to help out. She'd have to be a little crazy to take us on. Just keeping things clean was a major job. Our log cabin had a little kitchen and a Briggs & Stratton–powered washing machine that you had to kick-start like a motorcycle. Smoke would pour out of it and it would shake and shimmy all over the floor. If you weren't watching, it would fetch up against the trapdoor to the cold cellar, shake it open, and the next thing you know the washing machine would be roaring away and falling down into the root cellar.

Then the wrasslin' match would start! I was the one who was supposed to be watching the washing machine, and if Dad came in and saw the washing machine falling down the hole he'd give me a good lick, so I'd be jumping into action, trying to wrestle a big motorized washing machine full of water and clothes out of this trapdoor. Once the clothes were washed you'd have to run a hose out into the yard and drain the washer, and that would make a nice big pool of muck and suds in the yard.

The walls of the house were insulated with sawdust, and come spring the flying ants would emerge. I don't know where they came from. I guess they made nests in the walls, but anyway they'd be everywhere. They'd be all over the stove, in the frying pan, in the soup. Great big ones. I'm sure they had a fair amount of protein and vitamins in them, and we probably ate more than a few of them. I guess the ants were an appetizer before the porridge. We kept a twenty-pound bag of porridge in the cupboard. The mice would get in through the bottom of the bag. Then the odd bit of mouse poop would appear in our dish with the rolled oats. Of course, when boiled, mouse poop swells up to about half the size of a raisin. When cousin Tony came to visit he'd put lots of brown sugar on his porridge, close his eyes, and eat it all up. He said it wasn't bad as long as he didn't see the miniraisins in it.

Lying in bed at night I remember the mice would be running in the walls, right past my head. It was like having a freeway going past your pillow, scampering feet, one after the other. Every time I see one of those nail guns they have today I wish that I had one back in those days, and I would have given those mice a hard time. They acted like it was more their house than it was ours.

With all that, plus all the wild kids, the hard work, and the poor surroundings, it wasn't the sort of setup that would be irresistibly attractive to a whole lot of single women. Most women lived in towns and had electricity, television, phones, and running water. The only things we had were coal-oil lamps, storytelling, and smoke signals. But you never know what fate and good luck are going to send your way. One Sunday Herm Wald, a young fellow who was probably about twenty-five, shows up in our yard in this fancy white 1961 Pontiac two-door hardtop. He gets out of the car and shakes my dad's hand. "Stanley, I'd like to buy a bottle of whiskey."

"I've got no whiskey," my dad says.

"Oh, I know you've got one around here somewhere."

"No, I don't," my dad says. Meanwhile he's walking around the car. "Herm, did you go to church today?"

"No, I didn't."

"You should be going to church. You drink too much. You party too much. You should be getting yourself a job with Alberta Government Telephones. Make eight hundred bucks a month, get yourself a good pension."

Dad's walking around the car, preaching to Herm. "You're a good-looking boy. You should do something with your life."

Herm worked on the rigs and was addicted to a good time.

Dad's kicking the tires. "Who's that woman sleeping in the backseat?"

"That's my girlfriend," says Herm. "We're going to get married."

"I'll trade you a bottle of whiskey for her."

"Oh, no, I love her. We're going to get married."

"Well, no bottle of whiskey then."

Herm thinks about it for a while. "I'll tell you what, you take her, and I'll come and get her in the morning."

Dad says, "Herm, I don't think you understand. I don't want her for the night. I've got these kids here, and I need a woman to look after them, to help with the cooking and cleaning."

"Well, no, we're getting married. You can't have her for good."

Dad walks around the car a few more times and Herm finally says, "Okay, you can have her. But I want a full bottle of whiskey."

"You can't come back and get her. If she wants to go somewhere in the morning, that's fine, I will take her. But don't you come back looking for her."

"Okay, okay."

"Boys, come here!"

My brother Richie and I came out of the house and Dad told us to each grab an arm. She was out cold, so my dad took a leg and Herm took a leg and we skidded her out of the car and hauled her into the house and put her on the bed. It was probably one of the more ungainly entrances a lady ever made at our house.

Herm left with his bottle of whiskey, and I don't think the cows got fed the next morning because Dad got up early, to head off Herm at the driveway. He knew Herm would come back and of course he did. That big white Pontiac came down the road and turned into the driveway, but it didn't get far because my dad stood there in front of it. He had his fists on his hips and his feet apart. My dad was like a bantam rooster and when he took a position you couldn't budge him. Herm said, "I've come to get my woman."

"You can't have her."

"But I love her. We're going to get married."

"The marriage is off. You sold her to me for a bottle of whiskey."

"I'll trade you something for her."

"A deal is a deal. She's ours now."

Herm finally realized he was going to have to fight my dad to get her back, and my dad was not the sort of man you wanted to pick a fight with. So he left, and that woman stayed with us for more than a month. She treated us well. I remember this one time, I went into town with her, and we picked up the '61 Pontiac, which was in fact her car. When she drove it back the motor was screaming as she went down the street. She told me there was something wrong with the car, but it turned out she had it in first gear. The car had a two-speed Powerglide transmission. We shared a good laugh about that. Then she left, but that was to be expected. The only way Dad could find a wife who could take the hardship was to bring one over from the old country.

It Takes a Village to Raise a Little Polack

When you're growing up, it's not just your parents and relatives who educate you. Sometimes the adults and old-timers you meet in your neighborhood have as much influence on you as your own family.

We had a neighbor who lived in the woods called Fat Newton. My brother Richie and my sister, Simone, decided that it was disrespectful to call him "Fat," so we asked him what his first name was. It was Francis, and we were the only ones allowed to call him that. One day another neighbor came into the house and called him Francis and boy, he didn't like that. "Don't ever call me Francis," he shouted. "My name is 'Fat' or 'Fats' to you!"

Fat Newton had been a private during World War I and he had been a boxer, too, but he was just a stout guy. He had little hands and little feet and he was about five-four and weighed about four hundred pounds. He lived in a little two-room shack way back in the woods—single-pane windows, dirty floors, and a big old woodstove in the corner.

Most people talk with their throats, but old Fat Newton talked from the pit of his stomach. When he talked, the floor shook and the windows rattled. When you were telling him something his voice would get louder and he would get more excited and pretty soon it was like a volcano going off in that little two-room shack.

My brother Richie used to enjoy getting Fat all stirred up, so he would make up stories about stuff that he had done that day. He'd say, "You know what, Francis, I got three deer this morning."

"No!"

"Yep, with one bullet."

"NO-O-O!!!"

Anyway, Richie was really money-hungry in those days. He was always trying to make a nickel. He wasn't money-hungry as he got older but he was about twelve years old at the time and he would do anything for money. He'd go to my dad and say, "I'll eat that fly for a nickel."

My dad would say, "Okay."

Richie would pop the fly in his mouth and take the nickel. One time he made a dime eating a stickleback—that's one of those little minnows with barbs on its back. And one time someone offered him five dollars to eat a mouse, but I think Richie drew the line right there.

Francis used to chew snuff and spit it onto the stove. The tobacco would sizzle and go shooting around on the top of the stove.

I'd say, "Francis, don't you think that's a little dirty, spitting on the stove like that?"

And he'd roar, "Don't you know nuthin', boy? That's the cleanest thing you can do! The top of that stove must be five hundred degrees!"

Anyway, Francis saved the empty snuff cans and used them for storing pennies. He must have had eight or nine of them full of pennies. Whenever Richie was visiting he was always staring at those snuff cans, trying to figure out how he could persuade Francis to give him some of that money. He would say, "Francis, do you think I can have those cans of pennies?"

"I'll tell you what, boy, you can have them when you can carry those cans on the tip of your pecker!"

So Richie never did get those pennies.

Francis's cabin just had a rough wood floor. One day Richie said, "Francis, your floor is real dirty. When did you sweep it last?"

"Oh, maybe two years ago."

"Don't you think it's time?"

"Good idea, boy, get me the broom."

Richie found the broom and it still had a price tag on it. He'd never used it and it was about six years old. There was all kinds of stuff on the floor, nuts and bolts and different kinds of ammunition——.22s and .30–30s and .303s—and we sat there watching as Francis worked away with the broom, sweeping all that crap into a dustpan, two heaping loads. It was pretty dark in the cabin because Francis just had an old kerosene lamp. When he was finished he just opened the door of that woodstove and tossed it all inside.

Richie backed his chair against the wall and just grimaced. Francis pulled out his can of snuff and took a big pinch, and just as he was getting ready to spit on the stove that first round went off and Francis rose about three inches off that chair.

Bang!! went the ammunition.

"No!" roared Francis.

Bang, bang!

"NO-O-O!!!" bellowed Francis.

You never heard anybody roar so loud in your life.

That poor old stove took a beating. It must have been five minutes before the bullets stopped flying around inside.

There was another guy, an old character named Charlie Eddie. And it was Charlie who gave me my first vehicle. It was a '56 International stepside pickup with a 240-cubic-inch, six-cylinder motor and no brakes. Charlie was an old bachelor and he talked really, really slow-w-w. He used to make moonshine whiskey and he told stories about the police chasing him through the woods—good stories, but we had a hard time imagining Charlie doing anything quickly, let alone running.

Fat Newton once told Richie and me, "Charlie is so slow that a bear chased him up a tree once, and guess what? The bear beat him to the top."

Charlie went out hunting one time, riding on his horse, and he came across some moose tracks. "I tied my horse to a tree and took off on those tracks. I tracked that moose for two days and two nights, and finally there he was. I fired two rounds and he fell dead. It was kind of funny, though. As I was skinning and quartering that moose I couldn't help noticing it had a saddle on it."

Anyway, Charlie gave me this old pickup truck, and I used it to haul some firewood for Fat Newton. When I was finished he said, "You must be hungry, boy!"

Well, I was about fourteen years old and I got hungry just breathing, let alone working, so I said, "Sure, I could eat."

"Well, sit down, I'll fry up some horse cock."

I'd never heard of a foodstuff called horse cock, but I was willing to try it out.

It turned out to be a roll of baloney, about three inches wide and two feet long. I sat on this old army cot against the wall. He cut off this slice of baloney about three inches thick and threw it in a cast-iron skillet. It was all coated with grease and chunks of old food and gobs of charcoal and it was just disgusting. So I said, "Francis, don't you ever wash your skillet?"

"Don't you know nuthin', boy?! You never, *ever* wash a cast-iron frying pan, or you wash the taste right out of it!"

So he threw that slice of baloney in the frying pan, burned both sides of it, and tossed it on a plate and gave it to me. Well, I was hungry as the dickens and the first bite tasted pretty good. The second bite wasn't too bad, but by the time I got to the third bite it was starting to taste pretty rank.

I didn't want him to roar at me for being a sissy, so I nodded my head as if I was enjoying his green baloney; then, when he wasn't looking, I threw it under the bed.

Little did I know that his two cats were sleeping under the bed. They started yowling and fighting with each other over the baloney. Francis yelled, "Lift your legs, boy!!"

He grabbed this old .30–30 off the wall and swung it under the bed and whacked the cats with the gun, and they stopped yowling. Goodness knows what he did to the cats. Good thing the gun didn't go off, too, because he kept it loaded.

"I see you've finished your horse cock!" he announced. "Did you like it?"

"Oh, yes, Francis, it was great."

"Then let me get you some more. I've got lots here and you need to eat it up!"

He cut off another piece and I pretended to eat it. As soon as he wasn't looking I tossed it under the bed, too, but this time I tossed it to the far end of the bed so the cats each had a piece and they didn't have to fight. He turned around and my plate was clean, just like that.

Francis was real pleased and cut me another piece, and I kept throwing it under the bed, and I guess those cats had about two weeks' worth of baloney between them by the time Francis was finished serving my lunch.

Dad Does Some Dog Whispering

Our neighbor Lloyd Newton had a male cow dog that was very smart and well known in the country for his humanlike abilities with cattle. At that time, our cow dog was a female. Lloyd's dog would walk a mile to breed her every time she would go into heat. There was no demand for dozens of pups, so my dad would drown them. He hated doing this.

The next time she was in heat, my dad tied her to the porch. Lloyd's cow dog marched right in there. Dad closed the door and took out his straight razor and bottle of creolin. In less than a minute, Lloyd's dog had lost his testicles and had the cuts disinfected. The dog ran off home with blood running down his back legs. It was not a pretty sight. Well, after that, this thing was totally useless as a farm dog. It would just eat and sleep beside the food bowl and get fat.

Years later I ran into Lloyd, and boy, did he get mad when I asked him about his castrated dog. I thought it was pretty comical, but he didn't think so. He wanted to take it up with my dad, but my dad had been dead for ten years.

Farm dogs are not pets, strictly speaking. They are supposed to be working animals, and they earn their room and board by chasing off predators like foxes and coyotes, rounding up livestock, and keeping an eye out for strangers. They need to be aggressive and fearless. So my dad usually chose farm dogs that had some attitude—he liked German shepherds and shepherd-Doberman crosses, and our dog was tough. You'd sic him on a cow, and he'd sink his teeth into the cow's nose and stick to her like a leech. One time this cow of ours got mad at the dog, wouldn't go where the dog wanted her to go. You could see the cow thinking, *Why do I always obey this little bully? I'm bigger than him.* She lowered her horns and told the dog to buzz off. That dog grabbed the cow by the nose and she kicked him. Well, our old dog didn't like that one little bit. You could just see him growl at the cow. It was just clear as anything that he was saying, "Oh, so you want to play rough?"

The dog ran around and bit the cow on the tendon, sank his teeth into the leg that she kicked him with. The cow started bawling and tried to hook the dog with her horns. Well, the dog just growled again. "You'd rather get bitten on the face? Fine, take your choice."

The dog ran around and latched on to the cow. The cow started backing up, blood pouring from her nose. But wherever she went, that dog went with her. She had to drag him around with that dog's teeth sunk into her snout. You could see that look of misery in her eyes: *Okay, okay! You've made your point!* The dog won that little contest of wills, and from then on whenever the dog ran up to that cow she perked right up and did whatever she was told.

German shepherd crosses have that police dog attitude. They don't take any guff and sometimes our dog went overboard on the rough stuff. One time I sent him after a pig, and he ran up to the pig and grabbed it by the rear end and tore a whole chunk of ham right off the ass of this pig. My dad wasn't too happy about that. Another time Dad went to an auction sale and bought this old sheep for five bucks. It was an oddball, an old dry ewe that was good for nothing. He meant it as a pet for the kids, and we had fun taking care of her for a while, but one day our dog attacked this sheep.

I went into the garage and the sheep was standing there with a kind of stunned look on its face as this dog was tearing big chunks of skin off its rear end. The sheep had its head turned, looking at its own rump with not enough sense to know it had a problem. You see that all the time with wolves and caribou. The guys on the nature shows will always say, "The wolf will choose the oldest and weakest animals. That's how nature ensures that the herd will remain strong."

Yeah, sure. The way they talk you'd think wolves are a caribou's best friend. Well, it's not that way in real life. Not if you're a caribou, anyway. The wolf doesn't care if you're old or young or whatever. He doesn't check your birth certificate. That wolf will eat any caribou it can catch, and once the caribou is immobilized, the wolf doesn't even bother killing it before he starts to eat. The caribou will just lie there on the ground watching the wolf tear out its entrails and rip big chunks of meat off its ass. If all those wildlife shows on television showed nature the way it really is, mothers would be dragging their kids away from the television set and writing hysterical letters to the broadcaster.

So that's nature's way. And I was seeing it right before my eyes. Like all dogs, that German shepherd farm dog had some wolf blood flowing in its veins, and something in that sheep made the wolf come out. That sheep was just standing there not moving, looking at its ass, and the dog was grabbing its fur with the underlying skin and pulling it off. The whole rump of the sheep on one side was skinned. It was just bare flesh. I'm sure as soon as the dog finished skinning the sheep he planned to begin eating it. This wasn't the same dog that bit the cow and the pig. All our dogs were pretty wild. My dad liked German shepherds because they were aggressive, but they didn't live long because they'd either end up with a bullet in their head or they'd get run over by the trucks speeding down our gravel road.

So I was stunned, and I ran to the house to get help. "Dad, the dog is skinning our sheep!"

"It killed the sheep?"

"No, the sheep's just standing there and the dog is skinning it!"

Normally my dad would give a dog a chance to make a mistake or two. But in this case this dog had proven that it couldn't follow the rules. So he goes out there and sure enough there's the dog skinning the sheep. Well, he'll fix that. So the next thing, he goes into the barn and comes out with a .22 under his arm, the dog on a leash, and a one-gallon jug of used oil mixed with gasoline. And he headed off to the back forty.

We had twelve hundred acres of land, most of which was forest. My brother Richie and I were always removing trees and roots to create more usable land to farm. Dad walked the dog out to this big pile of roots we had gathered, put a bullet in that dog's head, and threw it on a brush pile. Soaked the whole works with gasoline and oil and lit a match. That was the end of that particular dog. Then he came back and decided to kill the sheep. You have to know where to shoot it, especially with a cow or a sheep, which has a tiny brain. You imagine a line that runs from the left ear over to the right eye, then another line that runs from the right ear to the left eye. The lines intersect on the animal's forehead, in a crisscross. That's where the center of the brain is. He put the muzzle of the gun on that spot and *whap*, down it went. Then he butchered the sheep and cut it up and served it to us for supper. This was our pet sheep. First the dog ripped off its ass and now we were supposed to eat it. That's life on the farm. We ate our pet sheep every night for the next two months. He made us eat it. I haven't really enjoyed eating lamb or mutton ever since.

My Short Career as a Cattle Rustler

Farmers generally do a good job of looking after their livestock and keeping the weeds down on their land. Every once in a while, there will be one or two who for a number of reasons don't. There was an elderly farmer named Jake who had acquired a lot of land during the Depression years and had cattle and pigs. He had gotten older and had trouble looking after it all, but he did not want to give up farming.

He wore railroad coveralls, the striped ones with many pockets. When he died, they said they found receipts in his pockets that were almost fifty years old. He was cheap but needed help on his farm. Few would help him for the ten dollars he would pay for the day's work. Dad would help Jake, herding animals, castrating, or hauling livestock to the Fairview Auctionmart. He would use his own vehicle and his own gas, and sometimes Jake wouldn't even pay him for that.

One night Dad came home at about nine o'clock. It was in the wintertime, maybe 20 below, and a moonlit night, full moon. I was about thirteen years old. In the Wild West that's when the Indians used to steal horses. They'd call it the "horse thief moon."

Dad came into the house and said, "Come with me."

"Where are we going?"

"Never mind, come with me."

We got in the truck, and off we went. I said, "You forgot to turn on the headlights."

"We're going to leave the lights off."

"Why?"

"Never mind."

My dad's driving always made me nervous. He was an even worse driver than my mother. Neither one of them knew how to steer a vehicle on ice or wet mud, and we were forever going in the ditch. So we're driving down the bush road with no lights and I've got my hand braced on the door frame because I'm fully expecting the truck to spin out on the next curve and maybe roll over in the ditch. I'm all tensed up, thinking, *What the heck is he doing driving with no headlights?*

We drive for a few miles. Park the truck on the road and proceed to walk off into this field. Deep snow, bitter cold. In the bright moonlight I can see that the field is trampled down with cattle tracks. And we walk into this bluff of trees, and my dad says, "Grab that rope."

"What rope?"

"Right in front of you there's a rope."

I look, and sure enough there's a good-size rope tied to a tree. "Grab that rope and hold on tight," he says. "There's a cow on the other end."

I untie this rope and hang on. Dad is hanging on, too. There's a good-size Charolais cow on the end of this rope, and as soon as we untie it from the tree that cow takes off.

Charolais cows are big and tall, like an elk. When the crops were nice and green, Jake's cattle would jump over his fences and make a loop through the all the farms in the area eating everything in sight. His pigs, too. I'd see a sow come out of the bush with a litter of pigs walking behind her, and I would say to my dad, "Where the heck did the sow come from?"

"Oh, that's just Jake's sow. She came five miles to eat our crops."

His livestock was famous for doing that, so people would occasionally steal one of his animals because he never paid crop damage. It was like collecting a debt.

As soon as we touched that rope the cow took off. It sprinted away and hit the open ground running full out, and when it hit the end of the rope, *whang*, I got jerked off my feet.

Of course Dad is hanging on, too, but right away he slips on the frozen cow shit and falls down in the willow bushes and lets go of the rope. This is his bright idea, but I'm the only one holding onto the rope. I'm falling down and getting up and he's yelling in Polish and giving me shit. "Hang on to that cow! You hear me? You're gonna get a licking if you let go of that cow!"

So I'm bouncing along behind that cow as it gallops across the field. I'm only thirteen years old, but I'm a big kid of about 170 pounds, and I'm pretty strong. Still, it's like being towed by a Jeep in third gear. I'm whacking against trees and bouncing off frozen cow pies and getting snow inside my pants, and I've got the rope wrapped around my wrists so that I can't let go even if I want to. This cow is beating the hell out of me, but I know this is minor abuse compared to the beating the old man is going to give me if I let the cow get away.

At the far side of the field the cow comes to the ditch. It's a deep ditch, full of snow right to the top, but the cow plunges in and forges through that snow even though it comes up to her shoulders. Then she runs across the road right behind the pickup and into the next ditch, and bogs down again in that deep snow. I'm basically skidding and tumbling behind her, but as soon as she hits the second ditch and starts struggling through that deep snow it gives me enough time to cinch that rope through the ring in the box of the pickup.

Now, try and pull a pickup truck, you crazy cow!

By the time my dad shows up, the cow is fastened securely to the truck and I've earned my passing grade as a wrangler.

So we've caught her, now what are we going to do?

My dad explains that we need to get her into the truck. That's not going to be easy because we've got fencing around the bed of the pickup and the tailgate is thirty inches off the ground. What are we going to do, lift the cow into the truck? I'm hoping that he's not expecting me to do it, because that cow is still fighting and thrashing like a crazy varmint at the end of the rope. I guess we got lucky, because my dad just touched it on the ass and it went sky-high. It jumped like a moose and went right over the tailgate and landed in the back of the truck.

So then we take this cow home.

Dad says to me, "Listen to me, boy, I didn't steal the cow. You understand?"

"Yes, sir."

"Do you know why we brought it home?"

"No, sir."

"I found a rope and it happened to have a cow on the end of it. That's my rope, so that's my cow. Earlier today, I was herding cows through the bush for Jake. I found a rope laying on the ground and I tied it to a tree so I could find it later.

After I finished herding, I realized there was a cow tied to the end of it."

That was my dad's story.

So we hide that big, rangy Charolais in the barn, and Dad goes and gets a pair of scissors, I think they're called pinking scissors. Those ones with little teeth going all over the place. And he goes up to this cow and takes the tags out off her ears and he starts slicing up her ears with the scissors, hacking them this way and that until they end up hanging in shreds.

For the next month or so he kept the cow hidden inside the barn. He fed it, fattened it up, tamed it down, and eventually took it to the auction sale. I went to that auction sale with him, and of course before the auction starts, everybody displays their livestock. Then they go into the auction and bid on them.

Well, in this case, the auction started and nobody was there. The auctioneer was asking, "Where the heck is everybody?"

It turned out they were all looking at Dad's crazy-looking cow. Everyone was asking my dad, "What the heck happened to the cow's ears?"

Dad said, "Well, you know what my dogs are like."

They all laughed because my dad's cow dogs had a reputation for being the meanest dogs in the country.

I don't think Dad ever stole a cow again. I guess he realized that he couldn't keep showing up with cows that had no ear tags and had ears like a Jamaican musician's hairdo. So that was the end of my short career as a cattle rustler.

My Short Career as a Professional Hunter

When I was young, about twelve, I did a lot of hunting. My dad would give me a quota of .22 shells and I had to be careful with them. We needed wild meat for food, and I would bring home rabbits and partridges. I also hunted muskrats and beavers for fur. I couldn't swim but I would wade out into the freezing water anyway, right up to my nose, to get the dead ones.

One time I shot a muskrat and I went in the water naked to recover it. There was still ice in the middle of the lake. I got halfway to the rat and my balls started to hurt so bad I had to go back to shore. I just put my underpants back on, then I waded out again and got the son of a gun. I was a long way from home on foot and needed to keep my clothes dry so I wouldn't get hypothermia.

Hunting got to be a little more challenging after my dad modified my .22 rifle by driving over it with his tractor.

It still worked just fine, but the barrel was bent and the bullets went way off to one side. If it had been a little more bent I could have shot around a corner with it! But I practiced with it and got a feeling for where the bullets would go. The farther away the target, the more the bullets would veer off to one side. You had to have all these angles figured out in your head, so it was definitely sporting.

I finally spotted a deer one day and crawled up within range. That was a real trophy, a lot of meat for the family, and I was pretty excited. I aimed about two feet high and about two feet off to one side and fired. The deer ran off and I thought, darn it!

I walked after it a little ways, just in case, and suddenly there it was, lying on the ground, shot right through the heart. Man, I was proud of that deer. The average person couldn't hit a barn with this gun.

One day in June, I came home from school and my dad said, "You know, the milk cow wandered off today. I think I'll go down to George Walter's place and look for it."

Dad made himself a walking stick and went down looking for the cow. George Walter's place was down in a valley, in a creek bottom, and there was nice grass there in the spring-time. Dad went down along the creek and saw the cow stand-ing in some willows. He came up behind it and whacked it on the rump with the stick and said, "Come on, let's get along home now."

Well, the cow turned around and it was a big brown bear! Dad was startled, of course, but the bear just looked at him and walked away. He came home and told me about it. I was excited about it. A bear!

Well, I considered myself to be a pretty good hunter by now, and decided I should go and shoot that bear!

A .22 rifle with a bent barrel was not going to be sufficient, so after dinner I cleaned the dishes and went into the barn and got my dad's rifle. I didn't ask him about the rifle because I didn't believe in asking any questions that could be answered with a "no."

His rifle was an old Lee Enfield, and it used .303 British am-munition. I put a couple of Savage .303 shells in my pocket, and any fool knows that the Lee Enfield takes .303 British car-tridges, and you can't use that Savage ammunition or you're liable to blow the gun up. But I never worried about little de-tails like that.

I was a bit of a romantic, or at least I considered myself one. It was my mum's influence on me, so I got my camera, a sketch pad, and a notebook. I intended to take a picture of the beast, sketch him, and write a poem about him. So I tucked everything under my arm and went off in search of Mr. Bear.

My plan was to do my photographing and sketching and poem-writing while he was still alive, preferably from close up, then proceed to kill him. That would satisfy both sides of me—the caveman and the poet. But when I found the bear, he was a lot bigger and scarier-looking than I'd expected, so I stopped about a hundred yards away, and decided to forgo all that sketching and poem-writing until after he was dead.

I lay down on this grassy knoll, lined him up in my sights, pulled the trigger, and *ka-boom*, that old rifle went off like a cannon.

I didn't realize it, but I'd shot that poor old bear right through the back leg and balls. He squatted down and shivered. You could see the heat pouring off him like asphalt in the summertime. Then he took off into some heavy bush. I knew this wasn't good, following a wounded bear into deep woods. But I had no choice. So I put another shell into the gun. It fit so badly that I bent it, jamming it in, but eventually I managed to force it all the way into the chamber. I closed the bolt, turned off the safety, and went stalking into that deep dark bush after that wounded bear.

Finally I saw the bear in this little clearing. He was sitting down, looking at me, and kind of groaning. The poor thing must have been in a lot of pain. I decided I would just walk up to him and shoot him in the head. Then I recalled that someone told me you should never shoot a bear in the head because they have such a thick skull that the bullet will glance off. I lined the gun up on his chest and pulled the trigger, but the bullet hit a little sapling between me and the bear and the slug ricocheted off and the bear wasn't hit. Now I was out of bullets.

The bear got up and started coming toward me. *Oh boy,* I thought. *Now I'm in trouble.* I dropped my camera and my sketch pad and my pencils and pens, scrambled up a dead poplar tree, and sat on a branch about ten feet off the ground. This was a black bear, and black bears can climb trees a heck of a lot better than any kid can, but I didn't know that then.

I guess the bear was too sick to climb the tree, because he just sat on the ground looking up at me. Shooting a creature in the balls is about the worst thing you can do. I wouldn't have blamed him for climbing that tree and ripping me to pieces, but he just sat there staring at me. After about three hours on that narrow, uncomfortable branch, getting bitten by every mosquito in the Peace River country, I decided I couldn't take it anymore, and jumped down and ran like the devil to Fat Newton's cabin. As I might have mentioned, Fat Newton loved bear meat, and I knew he'd be excited about getting a nice big bear.

I told Fat what had happened, and sure enough he was as keen as mustard. He got his tractor and his .30–30 and we went over to my place, where we took my dad's pickup. I wasn't allowed to take the pickup, but what my dad didn't know wouldn't hurt him. We filched the truck and went off and found the bear. Fat finished it off with his .30–30, then we skinned it, quartered it up, and hauled it back home, where we cut and wrapped the meat and put it on the deep freeze.

As it turned out, Dad gave me a licking for taking the truck but it wasn't such a bad deal because Fat gave me thirty-five dollars for the bear! And in 1966 that was probably about the equivalent of two hundred bucks today. A licking wears off, but money is still with you the next day.

After I sold that one bear I started hunting bears for Fat Newton on a regular basis. He would eat them up as fast as I could deliver them. There were so many bears in our neighborhood that I could always rely on Fat to keep me in pocket money.

Even though he was like an uncle to me, I was a little leery of him. Many times on the way back from hunting, I would stop at his door as it was turning dark. As I would go to knock, Francis would suddenly bellow, "Bullshit!" at a hundred and twenty decibels. It would scare me half to death and I would turn around and walk away. Turns out he had only been yelling at some comment on his transistor radio.

Often when I would visit, he would complain about all the baloney on the radio. When I would offer to get rid of the radio for him, he would give me a threatening look.

Old Fat always told me he wanted one favor in return. "When I die, stick me up in a poplar tree like the Indians used to do. But put a bucket over my head so the magpies can't peck my eyes out."

When he died they buried him and I always felt bad about that. I don't know how many times he asked me for that favor. More than a few times I considered going to the graveyard and digging him up and hanging him in the tree, but I never actually did it because I was too young. I didn't have the confidence back then. Today I'd do it for him.

2

THE OPEN ROAD BECKONS

"You've got only one life to live. Get it
over with or make something out of it."

My dad came over from Britain, where all he ever learned
to drive were tanks and armored vehicles. He was right
at home with horses, too, but he never really got the hang of
civilian cars and trucks.

I was born to drive. As soon as I climbed behind the wheel
of a car and fired it up, I knew that life would never be the
same. I was like one of those caterpillars that suddenly sprouts
wings and takes off. I never really cared where I was going
just as long as the engine was humming and the wheels were
turning under me.

Lloyd Paul

My name is Lloyd Paul and I went to school with Alex.

We went through all the stages of boyhood together—from wearing short pants to riding bikes in grade five to chasing girls and driving hopped-up cars in high school.

I remember playing sports in the gymnasium with Alex running around crashing into everybody and knocking them into next week. He grew like crazy when he was still young, and most of the time we were in school he weighed about 100 pounds more than everybody else. He wasn't a bully, though. He got good marks and read a lot of books, but you know what it's like when you're big and a little bit uncoordinated—some of the kids thought he was a dumb Polack, and we teamed up together for mutual protection. I was the skinny, mouthy one and he was my big buddy. If I started a fight, it was good to have Alex around to finish it.

As you get older, you start getting into trouble more often, and I don't know how many hours we spent in detention together. Even with that we were always working hard after school. If we weren't serving time in detention we were out hustling for a buck, doing odd jobs and saving up for cars. We really started letting her rip once we got our driver's licenses. By the time we were in grade ten we both had our own cars. We were pretty good drivers, but our cars couldn't manage to stay on the road. Alex's cars in particular would just as soon turn upside down as stay right side up.

One night on the night of the May Queen dance, Alex and I rolled his car three times and the only damage we did was break the fan belt. We had to drive around with no headlights because the generator wasn't working. But that wasn't too bad because we had lots of practice driving with the lights off. Finally, we went to this house where the toughest teacher in school lived. He had a car just like Alex's, so we snuck into his garage and removed the fan belt from his car and left our broken one in its place. We took a lot of pleasure imagining that teacher pulling out of his garage the next day and seeing that broken fan belt under his car, never realizing that the two students he was always tormenting had made off with it!

For a young man, a car is a major tool for growing up. When you are fifteen years old, you don't know your ass from your elbow. Your whole conception of the world is defined by what happens within twenty miles of your house. A year later, you've got a driver's license and you're like Christopher Columbus. You're out there exploring places you never dreamed about. They might be pretty boring places for a grown-up, but for a teenage farm boy they're as exotic as a foreign land.

I was branching out in other ways, too. They had these dances at the Legion Hall with kids who would come from other small towns in the area. It was a way of meeting kids your own age other than the ones you knew from school. All the girls were lined up on one side of the hall and the boys on the other. There would be a live band, usually one from the local area, and I met this girl there named Louise. She was there with her older brother and I asked her to dance. I was a pretty wild dancer and I guess she liked me, because we started going out together.

Her dad didn't think too much of me, and when I was sixteen years old he sent her off to Calgary to take a babysitting job for the summer. He thought it would get her away from me and break us up. But I had a 1959 Ford Meteor Sedan that I had bought for seventy-five dollars, so I decided to go find Louise. I filled the tank with gas and headed south from Fairview with fifteen bucks in my pocket. I was still in school, but it was summer holidays and I'd been working hard all day on my car, trying to make it roadworthy. This was a long, long drive, so once I got out on the open road I leaned my head against the doorpost and decided to catch a little nap.

The road was deserted and I was a wild-ass country boy, so it was no big deal to catch a few winks while you were driving. You just kind of snoozed and opened your eyes every quarter mile or so to make sure you were still pointed straight on the highway. If you saw headlights coming or if you heard gravel rumbling under the tires, you woke yourself up and drove a little ways with your eyes open. I could drive all night like that.

At one point, when I opened my eyes to check my progress, I saw flashing lights ahead. *Hmm,* I was thinking, *it's one of those pedestrian crossings. Some drunken bastard is walking home and he thinks he can just push a button and make me stop. Well, to hell with him. He can just wait until I'm past.*

So I put my head against the post and went back to my nap. Then I started thinking, *Wait a minute, those weren't yellow lights. Those were red lights. That's a train crossing!*

I opened my eyes again and now I could see this train going over the crossing. Straight ahead of me. *Okay, boy, enough napping, it's time to wake up!*

I jammed my feet on the brakes and laid down a streak of rubber that the cops later measured at 389 feet.

Blam! The car hit the train and proceeded to bounce sideways. It turned out that I hit the ladder at the front of the boxcar because the ladder sticks out a bit, and that kept the car from going under the train. If I'd hit the middle of the boxcar I would have gone under the train and I wouldn't be here today. The car was now sitting sideways and the train was going *bang, bang, bang, bang* as each freight car whacked the front end of my Ford.

I was a little startled by this development, so I sat there behind the wheel for a moment or two, trying to decide whether it was safer to climb out the left side or the right side of the car. At any moment the train could whack the car a different way and make it spin around, and I was liable to get crushed if I picked the wrong door. Finally I jumped out the left side and tried pushing the car away from the train. I put my shoulder against the car and pushed like crazy, and finally I got it clear. The end of the train went past and now I had some peace and quiet to evaluate the damage.

Well, okay now, it wasn't too bad, actually. The bumper was torn away, the fender was torn loose, the grille was all ripped up, and the clutch pedal had been knocked off the pivot so I couldn't shift gears, but otherwise it was perfectly good. I tried moving the car in gear, and even though it wouldn't start, it jumped forward on battery power and I managed to get it halfway across the tracks.

But then, what was this? The train had stopped about half a mile away and now it was backing up! Some guy on the train had seen me run into the side of it and now the engineer was backing up to see if I was still alive.

Quickly, I put my shoulder into the car and managed to get it off the tracks before the train could have another go at us. The train crew had called the cops and pretty soon the RCMP (Royal Canadian Mounted Police) arrived. This cop was not exactly sympathetic to my situation because some friend of his got killed at this crossing and he wanted to know why people couldn't see flashing lights plain as day. What was wrong with the drivers in these parts? Were we all blind or something? He told me that he was going to charge me with "undue care and attention while operating a motor vehicle."

Being sixteen, I was still pretty shy when it came to speaking to adults in authority, but I still managed to put forth the argument that it was a ridiculous charge. Basically, he was charging me with not noticing a bunch of flashing lights and a freight train. How could anyone not notice a freight train? The ground was shaking! The lights were flashing! If I hadn't noticed the freight train, then why did I leave 389 feet of rubber on the highway?

"You must have been going too fast," he said.

I told him my brakes failed.

"Then how did the skid marks get on the road?"

"They just failed at first, then they worked."

This was an older cop, and he'd heard every bullshit story in the book. But he still seemed kindly disposed to my situation. He said, "I'll tell you what. You go and make that argument to the judge and if he throws it out of court, no hard feelings."

So he left me with a ticket and off I went. The car wouldn't start in forward gear, so I managed to get it going in reverse and backed up a couple hundred yards down the highway to a service station, where I went into a phone booth, planning to phone my buddy Lloyd Paul.

I was going to tell Lloyd I was screwed. That was the long and short of it. I'd T-boned a train and my car was wrecked and I had a citation in my pocket and the only solution I could think of was Lloyd stealing his father's car and coming down with a tow chain to pull me home. But when I stepped into the phone booth, there was a wallet sitting there with thirty-five dollars in it with no identification. I didn't think God had left it there for me. Maybe that bad guy with the pitchfork did.

I took the thirty-five dollars and put it in my pocket and now my situation had changed again. Why did I need Lloyd? I was rich! I slept in the car, and the next day I talked the guys at the service station into letting me use their hoist. I put the car up on the hoist, fixed the clutch, straightened out the busted front end, and off I went, as good as new.

I had this stranger's money in my pocket. Thirty-five dollars was enough to live on for weeks. It didn't really bother me right away that I'd stolen somebody's money. But I began to feel guilty as time went on, and it still bothers me to this day. I wish I could find that guy and apologize, and pay him back with forty years of compound interest, but I never even knew his name.

After I got the car fixed, I was mighty happy, rolling down that highway with all that money in my pocket heading for Calgary. Hostile parents and train crashes were not going to stop me from finding Louise. I was excited about seeing her, and holy smokes, I'd never seen so much open country in my life. Towns going by I'd never heard of. Big trucks, fancy new cars, this spanking-new wide highway with a neat dotted line going down the middle, and not a single pothole or stretch of washboard gravel.

Somewhere by High Prairie, I picked up these tall, skinny kids hitchhiking. They were farmers like me, but they were about twenty-two years old, and for a sixteen-year-old kid like me they were pretty mature and sophisticated. The fact was, they were just as dumb as me or maybe even dumber. We were just this trio of morons heading to the big city.

We eventually got to Calgary and of course I was driving too fast. The speed limit was 30 mph and I was going about 40 mph. I grew up in a place where you just figured out what the road conditions would allow and then you drove about 10 miles an hour faster. Everybody drove that way. If you were driving the speed limit the cops would get suspicious because they'd figure you were acting guilty. But I couldn't help noticing that these city drivers were driving even more aggressively than I was. I mean, I was speeding down this road and all these other cars were veering onto the boulevard, driving right up on the grass, and going around mailboxes and lampposts. Some of them were even playing chicken with me, driving straight at me and then veering off at the last second with their horns blaring. Holy mackerel, what's wrong with these Calgary people? Are they all blind drunk at ten o'clock in the morning?

One of these farm kids was watching all these cars with a puzzled look on his face. He says, "That guy on the sidewalk back there just yelled something at us."

"Oh, yeah? What's his problem?"

"He says this is a one-way street."

"I'm only going one way."

We finally figured it out. This city was so big and complicated that they had streets where the cars just went one way. If they did that up north the town would empty out in no time. I guess you could blame it all on television, because we didn't own a TV and I had never seen cars driving in a big city. All these people veering over the boulevards and crashing into mailboxes watched television all the time, and when they saw this car with a crooked front bumper and smashed-in fenders speeding toward them they probably thought I was a lunatic escaped from prison.

When I finally tracked down Louise I found out that I had come to Calgary for nothing, because she wanted to break up with me. My rebellious ways had caused her parents, brothers, neighbors, and dog to pressure her into having nothing more to do with me. It was my seventeenth birthday, August 4, and that was my birthday present.

So I was feeling pretty low as I turned the car around and headed back home. By now I had squandered all that money and I was broke again. I visited this girl I knew in Red Deer and asked her which one of her neighbors was most likely to have a car with a lot of gas in it. She showed me a car, I siphoned the gas out of it, and back I went to Berwyn.

My Comeuppance

It's hard to tell a lot of these stories. A guy shouldn't be glorifying drunk driving, sleeping at the wheel, and stealing money. Especially if young people are listening. But I'm not telling these stories to make myself look good. I'm just telling it the way it happened.

Anyway, you never really get away with anything in this world. God has a way of straightening accounts.

When I got back home I was none too happy about getting rejected by Louise. I busied myself by fixing up my car. I took off the wrecked front fenders and replaced them with new used ones and a new hood. I didn't bother putting the grille or the bumper back on, but just painted the radiator and the front red and white. It looked like it had a big, wide, angry grin—kind of retarded-looking, you would probably say, but I thought it looked not only cool but pretty much expressed the way I was feeling.

Ronnie Markley was an acquaintance of mine. He was this haywire older guy from Grimshaw. He had a nice '57 Ford hardtop and his transmission blew up when I was racing against him. He didn't want to spend the money on another automatic and asked me if I would put a standard in her. I said sure, so he got all the parts and I went to work switching his car over from an automatic to a standard. I learned how to do all this stuff while growing up on the farm, where you can't just call a mechanic when there's repair work to be done—you have to fix the trucks and stuff yourself.

Afterward, we went to Fairview to celebrate the new transmission, and my buddies Tom and Fred Doll were along for the ride. It was nighttime, the end of summer. Tom started teasing me about Louise breaking up with me. I told him, "Hey, don't tease me."

"Louise kicked you in the ass, ha-ha."

"I'm warning you, don't tease me about Louise."

He just laughed. So I floored it, took that Ford up to her top end with that suicide knob in my hand. Do you remember those things you used to put on your steering wheel? That thing called a suicide knob? It was like a doorknob that you clamped on the steering wheel, and it allowed you to really crank the wheel hard.

When she hit top speed I took that friggin' suicide knob and spun the wheel. I really knew that car and I was accustomed to putting her in a sideways skid at a hundred miles an hour. When you're an extreme driver you learn that cars will do all kinds of weird and interesting things that normal people never learn about. For example, you can shift a rear-wheel-drive car into reverse at high speed and if you do it just right the wheels will start spinning in reverse and the back end of the car will do some interesting things. One time I had this old car with no brakes and I drove it for a week that way, just shifting into reverse and gunning the gas when I came to a red light. It gets some pretty funny looks from the other motorists, but it got the job done.

So anyway, I was speeding down the highway at a hundred miles per hour and I decided to pull one of these tricks. I knew just how to crank that wheel hard to the left so that all of a sudden you were going down the highway sideways. You were still on the road, but the car was sideways instead of forward. That usually got the attention of your passengers. Then you stomped on the gas and cranked the wheel over to the right, and a second later she was sliding down the highway sideways the other way. My intention was to scare the hell out of Tom and Fred. So I cranked the wheel hard and threw that car into a skid.

The trouble was, I had new tires on the car and I was accustomed to doing this little maneuver with bald tires. As soon as the car got sideways those new tires bit in and the car crossed the highway in a fraction of a second and hit the ditch backward and went airborne. The only other time I had that sensation was the first time I flew in a light airplane. I looked out and I could see the ground just flying under the car at a hundred miles an hour.

This terrifying sight made the adrenaline kick in and suddenly, *Boom!* My brain caught fire with the biggest friggin' flash you've ever seen, and I could taste ashes in the pit of my stomach. I've been in lots of accidents, and it's always the same. You see this gigantic flash, and you get this taste of ashes, probably from your heart stopping for a split second, and you summon up your old reflexes—*Turn into the skid! Keep your foot off the brakes! Put your foot to the floor!*

I jammed my foot to the floor and turned into the skid. But we were flying through the air, so of course that did no good whatsoever. We hit the bottom of the ditch and then we hit the approach with the culvert. Hit it sideways. That car decelerated from ninety miles an hour to zero miles per hour in four inches, because that's how much we bent that culvert. I wasn't wearing a seatbelt and when my shoulder hit the door, the roof support post bent. The door ripped open and I went flying. This all happened in a heartbeat. First I put the car sideways. Then I hit the ditch. There was a big flash of light and a taste of ashes and we slammed into the culvert. The door broke open and I went flying about 150 feet, hit the ground, and started crawling like a son of a bitch.

When you get in an accident you're in shock and you don't know what's happening. I flew out of the car and the next thing I was crawling just as fast as I could. I was practically galloping, I was crawling so fast. Then I stopped and asked myself, *What the hell am I doing? Why am I crawling?*

And I stood up.

It was August 23, 1970, and there was just a light summer drizzle. After the flash and the roar of the adrenaline and all this stuff, it was just so quiet and peaceful, with this nice little drizzle. And I looked up in the air and I could see the stars through the rain, and the grass was up to my armpits and I was standing there thinking, *Is this ever nice.*

Then I started thinking, *Where the hell's my car? Where are Fred and Tom?* And it dawned on me. *I just had a wreck.*

So I was looking all over, and then I could hear this slow regular *thump*, and it was the motor of the car. It was still running, but it couldn't have been running more than 250 rpm. It was just barely turning over, and every time it went *thump* you could hear the fan belt squeal. The fan was stuck right through the radiator, and the tie rod was wrapped halfway around the frame. It was just curled right around.

So I figured, *Holy shit*, and I run over there. Well, the Rambler seat had come out of the car and it was just sitting on the ground. And Tom was lying over the seat and he was just bawling like a calf underwater—*baaww*—and his head was split wide open. Your face will rip just like a pair of blue jeans, and his skull was showing.

Fred just had a little rip on his forehead.

All that summer I was wearing blue jeans, a T-shirt, and leather moccasins. For whatever reason, that's what I wore that summer. So I took my T-shirt off and covered Tom with it. I didn't have anything else and I was still in shock, so I was having trouble seeing. Fred was stumbling around, half knocked out because his head hit the dashboard, and maybe we all hit the steering wheel because it's pointing out the door.

Anyway, I looked around. I couldn't judge distance. It felt like looking through a jar of water—every light was a blur. I turned around and around—lots of farms in every direction. I thought, *Screw it, I'm taking that one.* And I took off for help, with ripped jeans, no shirt, and one moccasin. The first fence I came to I stepped in a furrow and friggin' fell through the fence and ripped my back open with the barbed wire. The next fence I grabbed the wire and tore a hole in my hand.

After running for about a mile I showed up at this farmer's house and beat on his door. This was one o'clock, two o'clock in the morning. He came to the door wearing a gown.

"Call an ambulance! I've got a couple of badly injured guys out there!"

So he called the ambulance. I went into his kitchen and stuck my head under the water taps. I was trying to wake up and wash the blood and dirt off my face at the same time, I guess. He went out there to take me back to the accident and he was so jumpy he tried to start three vehicles in a row, killing the battery and flooding each one before he could manage to get a vehicle started.

Finally we went down to the accident site and the ambulance was there along with two police cars. And there was nobody there. When I left them, Tom was lying on the seat and Fred was staggering around in the middle of the highway. I didn't like that because I thought he was going to get run over. But what could I do? I didn't think I could just stand here and babysit them. I figured I had to go and get help.

One of the cops said, "Where are your buddies?"

"They must have gone home. Or someone must have given them a ride."

"Come on. We're going to look for them."

We piled into the cars and took off. The police car in front, the ambulance behind, red lights flashing. After a couple of miles, we got to the Dolls'. They had this big kind of ranch house. As we pull into the yard I asked them to turn the sirens off. This was going to be bad enough already without all the flashing lights and sirens. The policeman and I got out of the car. He had got his big boots on, covered in mud, so I asked him to wait at the front door.

As soon as we went into the house I could see footprints in blood leading into the kitchen and into the bathroom, where the bathtub was half full of water and blood. There were bloody handprints on the walls and blood on the mirror where somebody was smearing it with a bloody hand. There was friggin' blood everywhere. So I thought, *Well, I guess it's no big deal that I've got a bit of mud on my feet!*

I went into the bedroom, where Fred and Tom were sleeping. Some guy picked them up and gave them a ride home. So I woke up Fred and told him, "Fred, we have the ambulance here. The cops are here. We need to get Tom to the hospital. His head's split open."

We got Tom out of bed and managed to get him through the bathroom, through the kitchen, and out to the ambulance. Oh, I was so happy we got out of there. And we never woke up anybody in the house, believe it or not!

When we got to the hospital the police officer came in and said, "Well, what happened?"

"I was going down the road, all of a sudden it just took off to the left. I don't know, like it broke a tie rod or something. That's all I remember."

"How much were you drinking tonight?"

My head was still going in circles from the shock. "Uh . . . two beers."

"You weren't smoking any of that grass, were you?"

This was 1970, and I read a lot of newspapers and magazines, but I barely knew what it was. "I've never even seen that stuff."

"Tell the truth."

"Okay, I have smoked a few things."

"When?"

"You know what rhubarb looks like when it has flowers on it? It's got that hollow stalk up the middle of the flowers?"

"Rhubarb."

"Yeah, about two years ago, I cut that stalk off and made a pipe out of that, and got a bunch of dried grass and leaves and I put it in there and I tried to smoke that."

The cop was just looking at me.

"I had a headache for three days."

"Okay," the cop said, and walked out of the room. He had decided I was just another dumb farmer. And maybe he was right.

More Lunacy behind the Wheel

I'm driving through Whitecourt one time in 1972, and there's a young woman in curlers standing by the road hitchhiking. She has curlers in her hair and a couple of bags of groceries in her arms. She climbs into the vehicle, not realizing that she's putting her life in my hands, and tells me that her husband is off working on the rigs or something. She doesn't have a vehicle, so she gets around to the store and so forth by hitchhiking. Fine, off we go.

The road was extremely slushy, with about six inches of snow on top of ice. There were these ruts running through the snow and the ruts were half frozen. If you got out of the ruts the car would start going all over the place. I'm driving like a mad fool just like usual, '65 Ford hardtop, and she's just talk, talk, talk. She was a real nice gal, and she was just talking away, over there on her side of the seat with a knife in her hand peeling an orange for me.

Neither of us are wearing seatbelts, of course. I'm going down the road at about seventy-five miles an hour, and as I pull out to pass this car I hooked the slush in the middle of the road and be darned if I don't turn crossways. I turn broadside, and as I go by this family, their eyes go as big as saucers as we go sliding past them. I thought I was going to kill everybody.

And this farm gal just keeps peeling the orange. She raises her eyes to look at this car passing us, turns her head a bit sideways to see what's coming at us on the road, then lowers her eyes and just keeps peeling that orange. I was going substantially faster, so I was passing them sideways, but she doesn't seem too concerned. Finally I got it straightened out, got my heart beating again, and she never said a word.

I say, "Sorry if I scared you."

She says, "Oh, no, I can see you're a pretty good driver."

I think, *Holy mackerel, this lady has a cast-iron constitution.*

Another time I pulled a girl out of a car that was going sixty miles an hour. She was a pretty young thing who had been captured by dastardly villains, and my brothers Richie and Mark and I decided she needed rescuing.

This happened the weekend of my cousin's wedding. I had rented a 1977 Cougar, which was a fast car back in those days. Whenever I rented a car the main thing I cared about was the size of the engine. I don't think I ever climbed into a car without taking it out onto a straight stretch of road and stomping on the gas to see what it would do. So we had this Cougar and it moved. Mark swore that he wasn't going to drink, but he got his hands on a bottle of vodka and by the time we got there his eyes were red and there was dribble coming out of both corners of his mouth and the bottle was empty.

These farm boys at the party were trying to spin dough-nuts with their pickup trucks. They would spin in a circle and the trucks would tilt up onto one side and then fall down and they would try to do it again. Richie was watching this. "That's pretty pathetic," he said. "Should we show them how to do it?"

"Yeah, let's show them how to spin a doughnut."

I punched the gas on that Cougar and we started going around, and around, and around, and big clots of earth were flying, ants, tree roots, rocks, all of this stuff was spitting out from under the tires and these farm boys were yelling at us. By the time we finished that whole pasture looked like it had been rototillered, and I just punched the gas, shot through the ditch, and gunned it down the road and out of sight. We were a long way from home, and there was no sense in getting into a scrap with a bunch of irate farm boys. Especially since we'd fought with some of their brothers before and we weren't all that popular with them to begin with.

So we were ripping down this dirt road, and after a few miles I spotted two guys stopped dead on the road lining up for a drag race. They were probably two hundred yards ahead of us and I just hammered it, heading right for them. They were sitting about four feet apart, but if you've ever been in a drag race, especially on a gravel road, you know that the cars tend to pull apart a little bit as they accelerate. The back end of a car will start fishtailing when you pour on the power, and guys are nervous about running into each other so they separate a bit as they come off the line.

Well, I was probably going eighty miles an hour as I came up behind them. Richie and Mark were whooping in encouragement and the cars separated just at the right time and we shot right in between, coming so close I almost took off their rearview mirrors.

We left them in our dust. Then, as the sun was coming up, I looked ahead and I'll be darned if there wasn't a Marlin, a turquoise one, driving along just ahead. It was probably the last time I saw a Marlin on the open road. It had big tires on the back and one tire was wobbling so badly it looked like it was going to fall off.

Richie and Mark were fast asleep, so I woke them up and said, "Hey, look, it's a Marlin! And it's falling apart!"

As we pulled alongside I could see that there were two young guys in the Marlin, about sixteen years old, and in the backseat was a girl. She was about the prettiest black-haired girl you've ever seen, and she looked very unhappy about being stuck in that car. The wheel was shaking, the car was swerving all over the road, and they were just laughing. I looked in the window at her and she just gave me this look, like, "Can you rescue me from these maniacs?"

I said to Richie, "Get her to roll down the back window, and help that girl climb from that car into ours."

We were right up beside their car, going about seventy miles an hour, and Richie rolled down the window and stuck his big hands out. If you could see my brother Richie, he's got great big hands and long arms, arms so long that his big hands would drag on the ground if his legs weren't so long. Anyway, the girl climbed out the window and Richie helped her as she gave a big leap and somersaulted into the front seat of our car.

It was one of those mornings where everything seemed to be happening. As luck would have it, she no sooner landed in the seat of our car when the wheel came off the Marlin and it went swerving all over the road and almost went into the ditch.

In no time, those guys were a little dot in my rearview mirror.

Meanwhile, the girl was looking at me, who she didn't know from Adam, looking at Mark, who smelled like a wino and had drool coming out of his mouth and looked like a werewolf, and I could tell she was worried that maybe she'd jumped from the frying pan into the fire. I just told her, "Don't worry, we're the Debogorski brothers. You're in the safest hands in the Peace River country."

She said, "Can you take me home?"

I said, "Where's home?"

"You have to turn around."

"I don't want to turn around."

"Please."

"Listen, girlie, it's four o'clock in the morning, and I'm tired and I want to go to bed."

"Then let me out."

"How are you going to get home?"

"I'll walk."

"You'll get eaten by a bear."

"That's better than driving in the wrong direction."

"Well, I can't just leave you on the side of the road."

"Then drive me home. I'll give you a beer."

So I turned the car around and headed off in the opposite direction.

She gave me directions and we ended up going so far back in the bush that there were trees growing across the road. But it's a small world, because it turned out that I knew her brother. So there you have it, one good turn deserves another, and we ended up sitting in the kitchen having a beer with her brother to finish off the night.

Mike Greenwood

I'm seventy-four years old and I've been selling trucks and cars all my life. If you come to my house in Edmonton you always see six or eight vehicles parked around it, in the driveway, in the yard, and my kitchen and living room are stacked to the ceiling with snow tires and air filters and auto parts of one kind or another. I guess it's pretty obvious that I don't have a woman in my life. And the city officials are not too wild about the way I live, either. They are always giving me a hard time about operating a business out of my home. They don't seem to care all that much about the guys selling dope in my neighborhood, though. Middle of the night, you hear the ambulances and cop cars going by. A gentleman across the street came home from work one night, and as he got out of his car some doper took his money and stabbed him in the chest. This poor fella had worked hard all his life, and ended up bleeding to death in his own driveway.

I've known Alex Debogorski since he was a teenager. He'd come down to Edmonton from the Peace River country where his farm was and I would get him work from time to time. My first impression of him was, *This is a strong, hardworking boy. He wants to make something of himself.* That was pretty clear. But he had a wild side to him as well. It's like he had two little genies perched on each shoulder, one of them was whispering bad things in his ear, the other was urging him to be good.

I got him a job painting the ceiling of a garage and it was so cold in there that he ran a car to warm it up and almost gassed himself. He drove an old Chevy with a telephone pole imprint on the side of it. I guess he had rolled it over in a ditch and the entire body was out of whack. Then he rolled again, the other way, and kind of straightened it out. It looked like an outhouse coming down the street. The windshield was broken so badly that he just took a hammer to it and cleaned it right out. You'd see him driving this old Chevy with no windshield. I guess he caught a few bugs in the eye at sixty miles an hour because he started wearing goggles, especially when it got cold. You'd see him driving around town with one of those leather helmets that the aviators wore in World War I, with goggles and gauntlets and a snowdrift in the backseat of the car.

He hitchhiked into town one day, soaking wet, with fifty cents in his pocket, and I said, "Sit down, Alex, we're going to make some calls and find you a decent vehicle."

"Get me a nice car," he says. "An Oldsmobile Toronado."

I told him I didn't like to see him driving cars. He was always wrecking them, rolling them over or driving them into immovable objects of one kind or another. I said, "Alex, you need something that will take some punishment."

"Like what?"

I had to think about that for a while. *What kind of vehicle would stand up to Alex's kind of abuse?* "You need a bulldozer," I finally said.

"Naw . . . too slow."

"Okay, a road grader."

"That might work," he nodded. "If you can find me one that'll do eighty miles an hour."

One of my best cars was a Chevy Impala. I paid $275 for it in 1971 and boy, it was ugly. It had a telephone pole imprint on the side and no windshield and my buddy Mike Greenwood said it looked like an outhouse coming down the street. He didn't think much of my cars, and was always trying to persuade me to buy a new pickup truck or something sensible. But this old Chevy ran like a hound. I'd roll it over a couple of times and then we'd just fire it up and keep on going.

One time my buddies and me went down to Edmonton to have a good time. We hit a few bars, and we were walking down the street, feeling pretty good, when one of my buddies started doing chin-ups on this overhanging awning. Another guy joined him and the whole awning came crashing down. The owner of the store came out and grabbed us and told us he was phoning the police.

We took off running and jumped in my car. We were racing down the street when we saw these girls hitchhiking. I pulled over, picked up the girls, and we sped off. Next thing you know, there was a big pile of sand and a hole in the middle of the street. I hit the pile of sand going about 70 miles an hour and flew right over the hole. It was like *The Dukes of Hazzard*. The girls were lying on the floor screaming, so I stopped the car and let them out. I was thinking, *First you want a ride—then you don't want a ride. Make up your mind!*

Anyway, that's how the windshield got smashed. It's difficult to drive safely with a smashed windshield, so I cleaned it out with a hammer. The cops would stop me and give me a hard time. That car was a cop magnet.

I'd say, "Sir, as a matter of fact we're just driving it to the body shop to get the windshield installed."

I drove it like that for months. Louise and I had gotten back together at this point. We were actually split up only for a couple of months. Her father couldn't keep us apart, so finally he just gave up and started accepting me as one of the family. I don't think he was too impressed with my cars, though, especially this Impala with no windshield. Louise would get wrapped up in a blanket and we'd drive all the way from Edmonton to Peace River, 350 miles with no windshield. One time we drove into a flock of birds and there were four screaming birds in the backseat.

Another time in 1974, I was driving along on a dirt road in the middle of the night with no lights on. Lloyd Paul was in the backseat necking with a girl. I used to drive it with no headlights because the alternator didn't work. It's not as hard to drive in the dark as you might think. The dark line on the right side is the ditch and the dark line on the left side is the ditch, and you just keep the car between the two. So I was driving along, Lloyd was in the backseat kissing this girl, and I went right off the T-bone intersection at the end of the road and Lloyd and this girl chipped their teeth on each other's mouths. It was a good car, but it had a hard time staying on the road.

Then there was the time Lloyd and I decided to go hunting. We were going to try and jacklight a deer, which means shining a light in its eyes, then shooting it. It's illegal, but it didn't work and we never tried it again. The Peace River country was the Wild West. Anyway, we were driving through the bush and suddenly we found ourselves up to the door handles in swamp water. I walked a couple of miles to a nearby farm and borrowed a tractor to pull the car out. I didn't ask permission. I just took the tractor. Tractors didn't have keys in them in those days, and I'd often just go borrow somebody's tractor when my car decided it was time to spend the night in the ditch. So we pulled it out, but when the farmer found out I'd taken his tractor without asking permission he was mad.

"Goddamn it, Debogorski, that tractor spends more time pulling you out of the ditch than it spends farming!"

He was probably right—he was a lazy farmer.

My Wild Brother Richie

When I was growing up my brother Richie was my main playmate. We had lots of fun together. My dad got us a sheep for a pet, and we would ride that sheep everywhere. The thing would be staggering along bowlegged, with both Richie and I sitting on it like cowboys.

Richie always had a bit of a wild side to him, but teachers and other adults were always easy on him for some reason. I always got in way more trouble than he did, even though he was worse than me.

Well, I think Richie got away with a lot because he's funny and it's hard to get mad at him. Boy, he's been in some scrapes. He's survived car crashes that would have killed anyone else. He would run his truck into the ditch at three o'clock in the morning on some deserted country road and fly through the air, doing end-over-end rollovers for two hundred feet, landing on the roof, flipping again and again. Unbelievable crashes. And he'd be wearing no seatbelt, of course, and he'd fly through the windshield and break half the bones in his body and a few months later he'd be walking around laughing like nothing had happened. "I don't have nine lives," Richie jokes. "I have nineteen."

He's got a face that's been rebuilt with steel and baling wire so many times you'd think he'd look like Frankenstein, but he's still a good-looking guy. I don't get it. Some guys watch their diets, take perfect care of themselves, and drop dead of a heart attack at forty-five . Richie has been trying to kill himself since he was twenty with booze and fast cars, but he's still as shiny as a new penny. He's had so many Native girlfriends he can speak fluent Cree. And he's always making fun of himself, so everyone likes him. He has a knack for talking his way out of trouble. But before you know it, he's back in trouble again. His main problem can be summed up like this—too many beers.

I remember one occasion when he was charged with impaired driving and had to go to court in Grand Cache. He hired an expensive lawyer out of Edmonton, a guy who charged a thousand dollars a day. This has always been Richie's strategy—don't scrimp on lawyers. And that's how he's saved his hide with all those impaired-driving charges. This expensive big-city lawyer won the case, and Richie got to keep his license.

So Richie and his buddies decide to go to Edmonton to celebrate this glorious legal victory. It's about a five-hour drive away. His buddies Fred and Tom Doll take their '66 Pontiac, and Richie takes his boss's Datsun pickup. When they get to Edmonton they go to the Corona Hotel on Jasper Avenue. This is one rough bar. On one occasion my other brother, Mark, was lying under the pool table while somebody was shooting a gun. There are bullets flying, glasses breaking. Even after the cops arrived he wouldn't come out from under the pool table, and they had to drag him out thinking that maybe he was the bad guy. My point is, this Corona Hotel is basically like a saloon in the Wild West.

So they go into the Corona and drink a bellyfull of beer. And after a few hours they leave the bar to see what kind of fun they can find. Richie has parked his boss's Datsun pickup truck in this vacant lot behind the hotel, and the other boys have parked their car out on the front street. The lot has a booth where you're supposed to pay for your parking, but at night there was nobody manning it and there was a chain across the entryway. When they all come out of the hotel the boys say, "Hey Richie, the cops are parked right next to your Datsun."

Richie looks at the cop car and says, "You just watch how I handle them cops."

So he walks over there, climbs in his Datsun, and fires it up.

The police drove Rambler Matadors in those days, with 304 engines and a low differential. So these two police officers are sitting inside this Rambler with their hats off eating donuts.

Richie gets into his Datsun pickup, puts it in reverse, backs it up about thirty feet, puts it in first gear, and just floors it. He goes right past the police car, hits this chain, almost tears the canopy off the pickup, breaks the chain, and roars out into the alley. The cops go nuts. All of a sudden it's completely *Hawaii Five-0*. Hats, donuts, and coffee are flying as they go after him, and by the time they hit the pavement their tires are smoking and sirens are howling.

Richie says that as they came up behind him he slammed on the brakes with both feet and just hung on for dear life. He knew what was going to happen.

The guys in the police car crash right into the back of his Datsun pickup, and the truck is going *chirp chirp chirp chirp* from bouncing down the road with this cop car pushing it. He shuts the key off and yanks on the emergency break. The truck is still moving when he jumps out and runs back to the police car. The cop who was driving has his face right on the horn, and the other guy's face is against the dash, and he yanks the driver's door out and starts screaming at the police officers, "Are you guys crazy? Are you guys on dope, are you drinking? You just ran into my boss's pickup!"

The policeman lifts his head off the steering wheel and starts blinking, like, What the hell?

The two policemen jump out of the car and start yelling at Richie. He's obviously had too many beers and they're mad. "Okay, get in the backseat," says the cop.

"No."

These city cops are rougher than the Mounties. They're always dealing with hardened criminals of every kind, and it makes them mean. If it was anyone else, they would bounce his head off the fender and heave him in the back of the car. But it's Richie, and he's being kind of entertaining, so they try to reason with him. "Listen, sir, we're not going to hurt you. Just get in the backseat."

"I'm not afraid of getting hurt. It's a matter of my legal rights."

"What do you mean, your legal rights?"

"Why do I have to ride in the backseat? Why can't I ride in the front seat?"

"That's the rules, so get in the car."

"But I'm innocent until proven guilty. I have as much right to ride in the front seat as any citizen."

"Just get in the backseat."

"I'll make you a deal." He points to one of the cops. "*You* ride in the backseat and I'll ride in the front seat."

"You cannot ride in the front seat. Is that clear? *Now get in the car!*"

Richie thinks about this for a minute. He frowns, strokes his chin. "Uh . . . screw you."

And he just starts to stroll off down the street with the two cops just standing there. Maybe they're still a bit stunned from the crash, because they don't do anything at first. And as soon as he turns the corner, he starts running. And despite the fact that he probably drank twenty-four beers that night, he can go like a deer. He's leaping over fences and tearing down back lanes and the cops can't keep up with him. Finally, he's lost them, so he slows down and spots a little tent in a backyard. He looks inside. It's empty, so he crawls into the tent and curls up and goes to sleep.

Next thing he knows he hears a jingling chain, than an animal sticks its head into the tent and grabs him by the ear. It's a police dog, and it drags him out of the tent, tearing off half of his ear. The policemen slap the handcuffs on him and they drag him downtown.

They take him to the city police station, some kind of a massive building downtown. Behind the sergeant's desk there is a room, a holding cell, all reeking with the smell of piss and sweat and puke, with a bench at the end, and a hippie, this big long-haired guy, passed out on this bench. Richie is getting kind of tired after all this excitement—driving all day, getting drunk, getting in a car crash, running for five blocks, getting his ear half torn off by the police dog, and now this. He is in the mood for a nap, but this friggin' hippie's got this bench tied up. Richie doesn't like guys with long hair—they offend his sense of what's proper. On top of that, this son of a gun is hogging the only bench in the room.

So Richie scowls at him, sits there for a little while, then decides he's going to do something about it. He gets up and starts peeing through the crack in the door. He's been drinking beer since morning and he's got about two gallons of fluid inside him. After about five minutes of this he zips up his fly and sits back down on the floor. Meanwhile a massive lake of pee has drained across the floor and gathered under the sergeant's desk. The old cop is so busy with paperwork that he doesn't notice. When another cop comes splashing through the puddle, they both look at the floor and give out this simultaneous roar of anger.

They rip open the door of the interview room. *"Who pissed on the floor!!??"*

Richie points at the sleeping hippie. "He did."

The cops drag the hippie out into the hall. *"Did you do this?"*

"I'm sorry, man, I didn't mean it!"

"You dirty son of a bitch!"

"I must have done it in my sleep!"

Well, the last thing Richie hears is this hippie wailing as they drag him down the stairs by his hair. Now Richie has the room all to himself, so he climbs onto the bench and goes to sleep.

After a while they take him to a basement with rows and rows of cells. And they put him in a cell there. There are quite a few guys in jail and pretty soon he hears, *Psst, psst.*

Across the hall, some guys are pointing at a cell where a guy has taken the blanket, made a rope out of it, tied it to the water pipe, and is going to hang himself. All the inmates are watching.

This guy ties a knot around the water pipe and jumps off the bed. On the way down he slams his knee into the bottom bunk and that kind of snaps him out of it. *"Ouch!!"* Suddenly he doesn't want to die anymore. So he's up on his tiptoes trying to undo the knot and everybody in the jail is screaming, "Die, you son of a bitch! Die! Die!"

The jailer hears this racket and comes running. He unties the guy's knot, takes away all the guy's clothes and bedding, and all night long the guy's teeth are rattling and he's moaning from the cold.

In the morning when Richie is discharged the guy is still naked and limping from hitting his knee. That was Richie's trip to Edmonton. He had too many beers.

Fighting a Bronco

When I was young, long before I became a respectable family man and a lay minister, I seemed to get in a lot of fights. My brothers and my friends were always telling stories about me, like I was some kind of wild man. But as I got a little older I began to realize that lots of times they were just putting me up to it. They'd get in trouble then I would come and bail them out, and it would end up looking like I had caused the fight in the first place. Often I was just minding my own business and trouble landed in my lap.

It was one of these situations that almost got me killed.

When my little brother Greg graduated from grade twelve, he attended a big graduation party at his school. After the party, everybody did the usual thing and headed off into the bush to have a bonfire. The farmer had given permission for the kids to use his land, and everybody was in a pretty good mood. It was just a nice gathering, everybody enjoying the return of the nice weather, standing around a fire, having a few beers, and having a good time.

As usual, the trucks and cars were parked in a long row and one car was pulled up near the fire with its doors open, providing the mandatory sound track of high-energy rock 'n' roll. The girls were flirting with the boys, the boys were telling all their usual lies and flirting with the girls, and there was this general feeling that one chapter of life was over and another was about to begin. You know what graduation is like. It's a big deal, but have a party, add liquor, and intertown rivalries come to a head.

Around three in the morning, just as the party was really getting going, a Ford Bronco came pounding into the pasture and pulled right up to the fire pit and parked. The guy driving the Bronco was a bad actor named Butch Mitchell, and he was accompanied by his little brother Spud and some other troublemakers. These guys were nasty characters. (Some of them had recently been charged with raping an eighteen-year-old girl.) Butch Mitchell, who was about twenty-one years old at the time, walked up to this kid named Chris Iverson and gave him a shove. It seems that Iverson had beaten his little brother in a fight a couple of nights before, and now Butch was determined to get revenge.

Butch and Iverson started fighting, but every time Iversen got the upper hand, Butch's cronies jumped in and kicked or punched him. Finally one of the bad guys smacked Iverson in the head with a wine bottle. Greg was a tall, skinny, good-natured kid and he was not equipped to fight with the likes of these guys. He jumped in anyway and tried to help out, but Butch's goons jump on Gregory and gave him a good licking.

Around this time I came roaring into the party in my '77 Trans Am, and as I pulled up to the fire, I misjudged the distance and ran onto a hay bale and stalled the car. I didn't want to look foolish, so I didn't put her in reverse and start spinning my tires and all that. I just pretended that I actually wanted to ram a hay bale. When you're young it's all about keeping up appearances. So I threw the car into park and shut it off. I had got no idea there was trouble brewing. I was just there to have a good time.

And I rolled down the window and my brother came up, and I couldn't help but notice that he was looking a little poorly on account of having a footprint on his forehead. You could see the bootprint right on his forehead, complete with the tread pattern. And his arm was bleeding because these goons hit him with a broken wine bottle.

I said, "What the hell's going on?"

"Well, these Mitchell boys came down from Peace River and they're beating us up."

"Why are they beating you up?"

"It's some kind of vendetta thing going back a month or so. Somebody beat somebody else up in Grimshaw and now they're taking it out on us."

"What do you want me to do about it?"

"They're wrecking our party. We'd like you to get rid of them."

"Where do you want me to start?"

"Him," he said, pointing at this guy standing across the fire.

This one Mitchell boy he was pointing at was a rough customer, with big arms, a criminal record, and a bad attitude. It was still dark and this Mitchell character couldn't really see what I was doing. I walked around behind the car and opened the trunk. It was pitch black in there, but I knew where the tire iron was, so I took it out, held it up against my leg, and started walking over toward him.

I said, "Come here, my friend, I want to talk to you."

Instead of standing his ground he started running for the bush, and I took off after him. Then I heard this noise and I looked over my shoulder and the other Mitchell was jumping into this jacked-up Bronco. *Vroom*, he fired it up and roared straight at me.

So I stopped chasing this guy and the Bronco charged me. I stood there like a bullfighter, waiting for the last minute, then, just before it hit me, I stepped out of the way and swung that tire iron right into the middle of the windshield, using every ounce of power I had.

The truck brushed against me and spun me around. My arm was up in the air, having bounced back after slamming the tire iron into the windshield, so I brought it down and took out the side window as he went roaring by. Well, that felt pretty good, so I threw that tire iron like a boomerang to take out the back window. The shot was dead on—it hit the bottom of the frame and broke the window and flew right up in the air.

The truck turned hard to come back and get me, and as he made the turn he hit two guys who were standing beside the fire talking to each other. *Bang, bang,* he whacked these two guys like stalks of corn. These two guys flew up in the air and landed in the fire. One guy landed on his back and the other guy landed on his front. I ran toward them, trying to save them, and wondering which one I should grab first. This fire pit is all full of coals and broken glass, and as I was running toward them I figured the guy on his back was going to be the slowest getting up, so I'd go for him. The guy on his front would probably just jump out of the fire.

Well, as I got to the one who landed on his back, he just jumped up like a squirrel and scrambled out of the fire. And the guy who landed on his face, he was just squirming in the flames. He'd been temporarily paralyzed from the shock of the truck and couldn't move, so I grabbed him and dragged him out and I rolled him over.

Just at that moment, the truck was coming around for another pass and it hit the guy who jumped out of the fire. This poor guy couldn't get a break. The truck hit him hard with the left front headlight and threw him high in the air, then ran him over, the front wheel and back wheel going right across his chest.

So now the truck was coming around again. I quickly extinguished the flames on the first guy, then start rounding up people, you know, women and kids, and stuff, "Get in the trees!"

Everybody was screaming, running for their lives. People were running into the bush, hiding behind the trees, and now the truck hit another kid and ran him over. Right away he climbed to his feet and started looking around in the grass for his glasses. He was in shock, Where are my glasses? So now the truck came back in a big circle and almost ran over him again!

Fortunately, his girlfriend grabbed him after the truck hit him for the second time and persuaded him to forget about his glasses and dragged him out of there.

The truck was coming toward the fire and I was thinking, I've got to stop this guy. So I started running toward the truck, head on. The truck was flooring it, coming straight for me, because it was really me he was after. I was running toward the truck with my bare hands, but what was I going to do with it if I caught it? If it was just a Bronco II, maybe that would have been no problem, but this was a full-size 4x4!

I looked left and I looked right, and realized I couldn't get inside or outside of his turning radius, so I just faced the truck, and as he hit me I slapped that hood as hard as I could, trying to go over the hood rather than under the bumper. Then he hit me in the midsection, hit me so hard that I put a dent in the middle of the hood with my hip. I shot up in the air, with my head above the windshield.

I could fill a book with everything going through my head at that moment. I was up there looking down at his face and he was looking up at me. It seemed that I was going to crash right through the windshield, and maybe he thought that, too—he didn't like that idea, so he took his foot off the throttle. I could hear the engine die for a split second. As I was hanging up in the air getting ready to go through his windshield I could see that it was a column-shift automatic transmission. His left-arm window was gone because I smashed it open with the tire iron, and I decided that if I rolled off the windshield I would reach in the side window. I figured that if I grabbed the steering wheel the vehicle would keep going, and if I grabbed the driver the vehicle would keep going, but if I grabbed the gearshift and put it into park, then it would stop. I was also thinking that if I did that, my arm would be stretched out and I would have no way to defend myself, and he would give me a few good punches in the face, but that couldn't be helped.

So I fell down off the hood, and as I was bouncing off the fender and hitting the ground I reached in through the window, grabbed the gearshift, and put it in park. In a split second the truck stopped dead, bang, just like that, and just as I expected, the driver was taking advantage of my position and choking the shit out of me. My throat was going to be sore for a week, but the truck was stopped. In fact, it skidded a little when I threw it into park and the back end swerved into the fire. So this was still a troublesome situation. The truck may be stopped, but I was getting choked to death and the back end of the truck was sitting in the fire pit with the gas tank sitting right above the flames.

At this point Greg came to the rescue. He came running out of the bush with a bottle in his hand and smashed that other side window open. There was someone else in the backseat, and as soon as Gregory smashed the window, that guy jumped out and took off running. Now the driver let go of my neck and got out. He couldn't go anywhere because the truck was in park and I'd taken the keys and put them in my pocket. The truck's back end was in the fire and now he was concerned about his vehicle. A few seconds ago he was running guys over and choking me, but now all he could think about was his truck. That's how dumb these Mitchell guys are.

The fire started going up the side of the truck. I yelled, "Let it burn, just leave the damn thing in there and let it burn."

But they got right inside this fire pit and started jumping up and down, trying to put the fire out and move the truck. I figured, *These guys are all half drunk and even though they were trying to kill us a minute ago I'm worried about them, too.* So I decided, *Well, I better get in there and help them put the fire out. Dumb as they are.* I got in there, jumping up and down, doing the fire dance, the three of us.

And the girls were watching, and after a minute they yelled at me because the fire was coming up under my jacket, coming out of my collar, and from where they were standing it looked like it was coming up the back of my head. Finally it got so hot I got the hell out of there. By this time some of the Mitchells had backed up another truck to the fire. They said to me, "Can we pull the truck out of the fire?"

I was thinking that pretty soon the gas tank was going to explode if somebody didn't move it. "Go ahead."

They hooked it up with a chain and pulled it out of the fire. When they were finished I went over to their other truck and took the keys out of the ignition.

One of them looked at me. "Give us the keys."

"No. I'll give the keys to the police."

"What do you mean?"

"The cops are on the way, and nobody is leaving until they get here."

All around us it was like a battle scene. This one guy was lying on the ground with a broken leg. It was folded over backward and twisted sideways, and he was laying there screaming, and people were trying to lift him into the pickup and he was screaming bloody murder. He was in tough shape. Finally they got him into the back of the truck and they went rushing off to the hospital with tires spinning. That's the worst thing about these parties, people get injured and guys start playing ambulance. They've been drinking and now they're doing their best to scoop up the injured and kill them on the way to the hospital.

Another kid was on the ground, fighting for breath, and I thought he was finished. He was just as gray as ashes and he couldn't breathe, he just gulped like a fish out of water. What happened was the truck ran him over and his lungs swelled up and he was having a heck of a time breathing. I got everybody to kneel down around him and we all said a prayer. Somebody found a blanket or coat and covered him up and waited for the ambulance, which of course had gotten lost on the bush roads. They didn't have cell phones in those days, and the ambulance couldn't find us, so somebody finally found the ambulance and guided it in. The paramedics scooped up that kid and rushed him to the hospital and he actually survived.

Eventually the cops arrived, too, and started hauling people off to the hospital and to jail. It was quite a body count. There were kids with broken bones and severe burns, and some were knocked unconscious. All kinds of girls were traumatized and crying uncontrollably, and by the time it all got sorted out fifty-one of these graduating students had to be treated for shock. Butch Mitchell, the one who caused the whole thing, was charged with four counts of criminal negligence causing bodily harm. It was more like attempted murder if you ask me. The fact that he didn't kill anyone was sheer luck. I guess the soft ground helped, too, although I doubt that Butch was taking that into consideration when he was gunning the truck into the crowd and driving over people.

3

TIME TO GROW UP

"There's nothing like failure to show you
where you fit in the world."

My mother always wanted me to make something of myself, to be a lawyer or an engineer or some kind of pro-
fessional. And I always got pretty good marks in school even
though I was a wild man. So in the fall of 1971 when I was
eighteen years old I enrolled in the University of Alberta, in
Edmonton. Let me tell you, not too many guys from my neck
of the woods went to university, so that was pretty good. Louise
was in nursing school in Edmonton, staying in a dormitory res-
idence, and I was studying hard myself, trying to live up to the
dreams that my mother had for my future.

Then Louise got pregnant with our daughter Shielo
and we had to make a decision. Well, for me, there was no

deliberation required. I loved her and I wanted her to be my wife. We were going to have a baby. It was all good. Her father never had much use for me, and when I went to see him he said, "She's too young to get married. We're not going to hold you responsible for this. You take off, go ahead, and we'll deal with it."

I told him it wasn't going to work that way. I told him Louise and I were gonna get married and we wanted the families to be a part of it. But I let them know that we were going to get married either way. I guess at that point he realized he had lost his long and hard-fought campaign to keep me away from his daughter, and they just agreed to support us.

We decided the wedding would take place back home in Fairview. Actually, we didn't decide anything. Once we told them that we were getting married the two families pretty much took over. They planned the whole thing. It was the middle of the winter and we were going to school down in Edmonton and all they did was tell us when to show up for the wedding. That's the way it worked in those days.

We didn't have a cent between us, but we were lucky because the families put it all together. My Auntie Lala made a beautiful wedding dress for Louise. My only job was to deliver it. Louise went up before me to attend the bridal shower and do all those girly things to get ready for the wedding.

Louise Debogorski

Alex and I were high school sweethearts. We met at a town dance in the Fairview Legion Hall.

We had our obstacles, like everyone. My dad didn't like Alex. He thought he drove too fast and wasn't good enough for me. He thought Alex was on the wild side, like way over on the wild side! When I was sixteen, Dad sent me down to Calgary to babysit for the summer, hoping that would break us up, but we couldn't stay away from each other.

When we were both eighteen, we were living in Edmonton and going to school and trying to make something of ourselves. Then I got pregnant and Alex said, "We're getting married."

There was never any question in his mind about it. And he went to see my dad and had a difficult conversation with him and settled the matter. But a lot of years went by before he told me about the time that he talked to my dad.

I didn't know a thing about getting married. I'd never done it before! In those days, your dad forked over for the wedding and everybody in both families helped out. So we were lucky and it worked out wonderfully. Alex's Auntie Lala made me a beautiful dress and I remember how special I felt when the ladies all fussed over me and helped me get ready.

It was January 28, 1972, very cold, but I picked green as the color of a new beginning. We danced all night, more dances that I've had with Alex before or since, and we both now agree it was the best wedding party we've ever been to. Down at the end of the street in Fairview there was this pink motel called the Flamingo. It had a big flamingo out in front and my girlfriends and I used to marvel at this big bird when we were little kids. When the wedding party was over, Alex and I went down to the Flamingo and had our one-night honeymoon. We had never stayed in a hotel or motel before, so we thought it was quite an adventure.

Eighteen years later Alex drove down to Florida for a little break. He likes doing that. He'll just jump in a car and go. He put some bullhorns on the front of his big old Cadillac and took off for a couple weeks. We had six kids, so I stayed home. He phoned me from Florida and told me he missed me. "Why don't you jump on a plane and come down here and see me?"

I reminded him that we had six kids and I couldn't just disappear. But Alex is not the sort of person who takes no for an answer. So I scrounged around and managed to find friends who would watch my kids for a week, and I flew down to see him. We went to Disney World and spent hours standing in line to go on rides. It was just like we were teenagers again. I told Alex, "Let's call this the honeymoon we never had."

Auntie Lala gave me the wedding dress in a neat cardboard box and all I had to do was get it up to Fairview in one piece and not be late for the wedding.

I was driving this '63 Acadian and wouldn't you know, I had mechanical problems on the way home. The truth is, I was driving a little too fast. This car only had a small engine in it, and I blew the engine between Whitecourt and Fox Creek. So there I was sitting on the side of the road in a dead car at 30 degrees below zero.

I was dressed like most silly kids are when they're eighteen or nineteen—light jacket, skinny shoes, and blue jeans. So I got out on the side of the road and started hitchhiking with this big box under my arm with my wife's wedding dress in it. I guess it made a pretty good story for the people who picked me up. Here's this kid with the wedding dress on his lap, looking at his watch because he's worried he's going to miss his own wedding.

I hitchhiked home with this wedding dress, then I conned my uncle into lending me a car for the wedding.. It would be kind of bad to make your wife hitchhike to her own honeymoon.

The wedding took place at the Legion Hall in Fairview, Alberta, the same place we met, come to think of it. I'm not sure of the actual date because I get confused over which day is her birthday and which is our anniversary.

My dad never drank much. Every once in a while he went for a few drinks at the Legion and he would be sick for three days afterward. Anyway, he decided to have a few drinks at the wedding about midnight, but by then we had run out of booze. My dad got this idea in his head that Louise's side of the wedding party drank most of it, and he said my father-in-law had hidden the rest so he could drink it himself. My dad was pissed off that he had finally decided to have a drink just when the booze was all gone. So the wedding could have wound up in a brawl, but it all worked out peacefully, more or less.

Then I quit school and we moved back to the Peace River country. I worked pretty hard, but I was just nineteen and still pretty wild. Because my mum died when I was young, I never really had much experience watching my parents work together as a couple. My dad pretty much ran the show. After I got married to Louise I figured that I would do pretty much the same—I would carry on acting like a teenager, doing whatever I pleased, and she would just go along with it. Well, any of you guys who are married know that life doesn't quite work that way.

Back home when my buddies and I weren't working, we were carousing and carrying on. My buddies enjoyed provoking the situation, of course, and I was pretty much being pulled in two different directions at once. They wanted to carry on with our wild ways and Louise wanted me to grow up and be a husband. The worst thing was when we went to parties. That's when the fights would start, and often my buddies would start them. They didn't want to actually fight, of course. They just wanted to watch.

My Short Career as an Oil Rig Worker

There's something in men that likes to fight. It's pretty pathetic. You don't have to look at the six-o'clock news—with wars tearing up the world from one end to another—you only have to walk down to the local bar, where you'll see otherwise sensible grown men suddenly trying to kill each other just because one guy bumped into the other. I worked as a bouncer once and I saw it firsthand. Totally normal guys have some kind of ingredient inside them that turns them into maniacs as soon as you add alcohol.

When I was working on the oil rigs I met my match. Oil riggers are pretty wild guys, and of course when they've had a few drinks they're even wilder. My buddies had a run-in with this tough fella named Dwayne Baker, and they told Dwayne Baker and his pals that they were going to get some reinforcements and come back to kick his butt. Well, it turned out that their reinforcement was me. I told them, "What did you do that for? I don't even know this guy!"

I wasn't too pleased. But it was too late, the fight was already arranged. So we went to this party, and sure enough, about eleven o'clock Dwayne Baker and his friends walked in, all ready to have this brawl. And this Dwayne was one tough customer. He was built like a donkey. And he loved to fight.

Win, lose, or draw, it was all the same to him. He was not the sort of person you wanted to go bare knuckles with.

I'd already resigned myself to the fight, and I figured the best defense is a good offense. So as soon as Mr. Baker walked in I started throwing wisecracks at him. And he was giving it right back to me. But it seemed I was a little better with my mouth than he was, and before you know it he got frustrated and hit me right in the yap.

As I was falling I reached out to grab something, and as luck would have it I grabbed him by the collar, flipped him, and ended up behind him, punching him in the head. It looked like a pretty cool move, but it was purely accidental. The back of the head is a very poor place to punch somebody. You can stun them if you do it hard enough, but oh, my hands were hurting and I was thinking, *I'm going to break my hands if I keep on doing this.*

So we started wrestling, and he drove me out of the living room and into the bathroom, where as luck would have it, he fell into the bathtub with me on top of him. You're in a lot of trouble if you're in a bathtub with someone on top of you because it's slippery in there and you're not getting up. I used to chew Copenhagen in those days, and when he punched me a couple of good ones in the face there was snuff coming out my nose and mouth. So I turned on the taps and washed the snuff off my face and let the water rise until it was up to his ears. I was sitting on him watching the water rise, and his guys yelled, "Don't drown him!" so I let him up. He thanked me for not drowning him and shook my hand.

So he went off, no hard feelings, and a couple of months later, what do you know, we ran into each other again at a party. Dwayne Baker and his buddies were having a party down at those shacks at Beaver Drilling where they worked, and when I showed up at the party, he made a few rude comments and gave me a shove. I went reeling back against the door, the door flew open, I went backward down the stairs and into the mud. Down the stairs comes Dwayne and he started whaling on me with his fists. As I mentioned, Dwayne was a good fighter, and this time our fight went something like this—he hit me in the mouth, I took three swings at him and missed. He hit me in the mouth, I took three swings at him and missed. After getting pummeled for a while I got tired of it and decided to step back. At that point I realized I had no ankle. I had broken my ankle in the somersault down the stairs.

I couldn't fight with a broken ankle, so I started crawling toward my car. All Dwayne's buddies lined up and started kicking me in the ribs with their steel-toed boots as I crawled toward my little Toyota Corolla. It was like running a gauntlet. I was a mess of boot kicks from my ass to my armpits. And to top it off, when I climbed into the car they started kicking it, too, and they managed to put a couple of dents in the fenders. I thought that was a little excessive.

I drove myself to the hospital and limped in and told the nurse I'd broken my ankle. She told me to go and sit down and she'd call the doctor. About three hours went by and still no doctor. I was sitting in the waiting room in terrible pain, and it was now three o'clock in the morning and I was thinking, *Hmm, this isn't very good.* I was wearing a brand-new pair of cowboy boots that I'd just bought for eighty dollars and my foot was so swollen I couldn't walk. So I got into the wheelchair and wheeled myself down to the nursing station and asked her where the doctor was. It turned out she hadn't bothered calling him. I was just a young guy and I guess she was accustomed to drunken rig workers coming in all beaten up and she's just hoping I'll fall asleep or go home or something.

So finally she called Dr. Schneider and he got out of bed and came down to the hospital to look at my ankle. He came into the examination room with the nurse. This same nurse was later killed in a plane crash, as a matter of fact, but that's another story. Dr. Schneider jerked and pulled off my brand-new cowboy boot to see what all my fussing and complaining was about. He took one look at my swollen foot and said, "My goodness, boy, you've broken your ankle!"

"That's what I keep telling everybody!"

Dr. Schneider was later murdered, as a matter of fact, but that's also another story. So he fixed me up with this big cast. Limping around on crutches, I was no good for working on a drill site, so that was the end of my career in the oil patch.

My Short Career as a Coal Miner

When the ankle healed after the fight with Dwayne Baker I went back to work. Nowadays it's hard to find a job, but this was the early 1970s and there were jobs everywhere for a young man who wanted to work. I was still a teenager, and over the next year I held at least seven or eight jobs, each one better than the last.

I worked for Canuck Construction, a company hooking up wellheads out of Fairview, Alberta, and I worked for Century Geophysical, a seismic surveying company out of Zama City north of High Level, Alberta. I also worked for Seisform Geophysical up in the high Arctic on Richards Island. At that place, by the way, one of the guys was killed by a polar bear. The bear jumped on this fellow with no warning and the crew boss had to use a bulldozer to drive the bear away from the body. The bear wanted to claim his kill and the crew boss had to intimidate the polar bear with the only thing on hand bigger and stronger than a bear and that was a Caterpillar D8.

One of my jobs was at K & L Tire in Grimshaw, Alberta. In 1971 this fellow came in looking for a truck driver to drive a dump truck in Grande Cache, hauling coal. He was in a panic because they had lost their truck driver and he asked me if I knew how to drive a truck. I told him I had driven a grain truck on the farm and I thought I could drive the dump truck for him. I told him I didn't have a license to drive a big truck, but they didn't think I needed a license because it was right on coal mine property.

I liked driving things, and I wanted that job. I wanted it bad. I was driving a '67 Coronet 500 with a 383 four-barrel carburetor with a four-speed on the floor. It burned a lot of gas and I needed money. Plus I had a brand-new baby girl named Shielo and a wife. This job would pay three times as much as I was getting at the tire shop, so off I went to Grand Cache to drive a coal truck and make some serious cash.

When you were a rookie driver on the coal trucks they would test you out first by putting half a load on board and then put you behind the wheel with an experienced driver beside you to see if you could handle the truck. I don't think I had ever driven a diesel engine before, and I had never used a Jacobs brake. Now, the lead driver was glad to have me in the truck because as it turned out he and his wife had been partying the night before. They had driven home and they had both gone to sleep in the car in front of the house. The bus that was supposed to take him to work had driven up and blown its horn. He had gotten out of the car and jumped on the bus and now that he was at work with me, feeling rather hung over, he had realized that he still had the keys to the house. He was a little worried about that because he had left his wife sleeping in the car with no keys to the house. On top of that, he was feeling rough, so he was happy to sit in the passenger seat and let me do the work. I guess I didn't scare him that bad and I wound up driving a coal truck there for two years.

I worked lots of hours in the mine, every bit of overtime I could get. I drove the foreman nuts.

Here's me arriving for work in the morning: "Is there any overtime?"

"Yeah, if you want it."

Here's me leaving at the end of the day: "Is there any overtime?"

"Debogorski, you're a broken record."

We were working ten-hour shifts, two hours between shifts. He just got tired of listening to me, so he'd give me little jobs to fill the time between. "Take the water truck, go up to the water hole. I don't care what the hell you do. Just sit there and don't miss the shift change. Make sure you make the bus in two hours."

On days off, I'd go and carry on and get drunk and party, but if they gave me work, I wouldn't go anywhere. I'd just stay there and work myself to death.

And the work conditions! If you've never seen an open-pit coal mine you have to imagine a big hole in the side of a mountain where all the soil and all the machinery and all the people are black. My skin was black, my clothes were black, the truck was black, and it was *hot*, as hot as Las Vegas in the summertime. That black coating of coal dust just soaks up the heat and you're always filthy, black, and thirsty. You can't wear goggles because they get steamed over as you're breathing, so you can't see a thing. The coal dust is blowing right up into your face. Your nose is plugged up, so you can't breathe through it, and you're inhaling coal right into your lungs. The coal gets in your eyes and you're in such pain that you feel like there's sand inside your eyes. I'd just push on, almost in tears, and I'd be thinking, *Why am I working overtime when I hate this place?*

Oh, boy, that open-pit mine was a dirty place. And dangerous, man, I can't tell you. The drivers are going up and down these steep roads in these enormous Kenworth and Hayes off-road trucks with thirty-yard dump boxes. These are body jobs. Loaded, they can weigh over fifty tons. The drivers are a mixture of all ages, but some of us are young, wild, and think we're hard to kill, but we get killed anyway, and fairly regularly. You could miss a shift and find yourself riding fifty tons of coal down a mountain going maybe a hundred miles an hour.

So you have to be a bit of a caveman to tolerate this kind of work. They say a woman has to be twice as good as a man to be accepted as an equal, and maybe there's some truth in that. One day this brave gal made a mistake, like everybody does sooner or later. She missed a shift or something, and the truck got away on her.

Maybe the average guy would have bailed out of that runaway truck. But I guess she thought that because she was a woman she had to prove something, and she fought that truck all the way down the hill to her death.

If You Go Down in the Woods

So truck driving on the coal pile was tough, dangerous work, and when we had a free night we were ready to blow off some steam.

One night in 1975 after work about five of us were sitting around having a couple of beers when one of the guys suggested that we go find some bears. We didn't have any specific idea what we were going to do with them, but usually when you find a bear you've found entertainment.

In those days Grand Cache was full of bears, and probably still is. You'd be sitting in the bar on a hot summer night and the bartender would keep the doors open to let in some cool night air and a bear would walk right into the bar. I'm serious—you'd look and see a bear come in the back door, walk along the back wall, and go out the front door. Oh, it was hilarious. You'd come out of the bar at night and they'd be walking down the sidewalk. It was not unusual to start your truck and pull out of the parking lot and you'd be bumping bears in the rear end so they would get out of your way. One night I was walking home, half cut, and I decided to take a pee against a fence. Well, just as I'm peeing this bear comes running full speed right toward me. These kids had given this bear a fright and it was running like hell and I had to move quickly and get myself zipped up or this bear would have run right over me.

So on this particular night, as it was getting on to dusk, about eleven o'clock on a nice summer evening, we're arguing about the best place to find a bear. If we had stayed right where we were, a bear would probably come walking past at any moment. But the best place was the dump. There were always at least a dozen bears at the Grand Cache dump.

So off to the dump we go. It never really gets dark in the summer, so even though it's the middle of the night it's daylight. The dump is a big pile of garbage in a pit about forty feet high. People usually drive up to the top and throw their garbage down the hill, and they all stand there for a while and watch the bears. On a typical weekend you'll see half a dozen vehicles up there, full of kids and the grandparents and everyone else watching the bears. It's what some folks do at Grand Cache instead of going to the drive-in movie.

So we pull into the dump, but instead of going up to the top we drive through the woods and come out at the back of the mountain of garbage. Sure enough, there's about thirty bears there. It looks like a Rotary Club convention. When you just see a couple of bears, they look pretty much the same. But when you get a whole mob of bears all together like that you can see they're all different. There's skinny ones, fat ones, old ones, young ones, and they're all snuffling around in the garbage like they're at a picnic. Well, by now we've drunk a lot of beer and we're full of bright ideas. Someone suggests that we should bail out of the truck and chase them. We're all nineteen years old and equally stupid, so we decide that's a great idea.

So we bail out and take off after them. The bears don't want to leave all that nice garbage, so they run in circles, wearing us out. This one 400-pound bear goes climbing up a tree and looks down at us, like it's a game of tag. The tree is so skinny that it's flexing like a bow under the weight of the bear. We start pushing the tree, and it goes back and forth like a spring and finally the bear goes *sproing,* flies out of the tree, and almost lands on top of us.

It's hard work, running around in knee-deep garbage chasing bears, so every once in a while we get tuckered out and take a breather, sit on the tailgate, and have a few beers. And the bears take a breather, too, sitting down and puffing and eyeing us like they're on the opposite football team. This is so entertaining that we keep it up for hours. By now it's breakfast time, Sunday morning, and we don't have to work, so we figure we might as well hang around the dump and enjoy ourselves. Every once in a while a truck pulls in and throws down their garbage, but we're not paying much attention because we're having too much fun. We keep trying different games with the bears, until I get the idea that one group of us should get the bears running in one direction, and the other group should get them going the other way. If we can coordinate all the bears, maybe we can get something going around in intersecting circles like the Musical Ride, which is this coordinated horseback exhibition our national police force puts on.

Well, we form up in two groups and charge the bears, waving sticks, but instead of going in different circles, they hit that wall of garbage and go straight up—thirty bears going up the mountain of garbage like a bunch of squirrels. Then, a few seconds later, there's an outburst of shouting and screaming from the other side of the hill. Slamming doors, honking horns, roaring engines.

We thought we had the dump all to ourselves. What's all the noise?

The next day I'm sitting in the bar having a few beers when in walks this older gentleman who's kind of a pillar of the community. I don't know him all that well, but I know him a little bit. He says hello and sits down and after a few minutes of idle banter he starts telling me this story. "You know, Alex, yesterday after church I decided I would take the old folks and the kids to the garbage dump to see the bears. There's usually quite a variety of them there, and the family enjoys it. Do you ever go to the dump to see the bears, Alex?"

"Well, yes," I tell him. "I've been there once or twice."

"It was kind of odd yesterday, because when we parked the vehicle there wasn't a bear in sight. We got out and looked around and the kids started asking me, 'Daddy, where did all the bears go?' I didn't know what to tell them, but then suddenly there was all this noise and suddenly, this great galloping herd of bears came storming up over the crest of the hill and charged right for us. It was the most terrifying thing you ever saw. My wife started screaming, the kids were wailing, and the dogs were running for their lives. There were bears everywhere. One bear almost ran me over. I just managed to get the kids and the old folks into the car before a bear jumped right over the hood of the car. Craziest thing I've ever seen. Did you ever hear of bears acting that way?"

"No, sir, I haven't."

"Are you sure?"

"No, sir, that's definitely the strangest example of bear behavior I've ever heard."

If someone were to ask me that question today I would say, "Global warming."

"So you don't have any explanation of why a perfectly normal group of garbage bears would charge a peaceful, church-going family?"

I kept acting like I'd never heard of such a thing, and finally he satisfied himself and left. I don't think he had any proof that I was involved in riling up the bears. But Grand Cache was a small community, and I guess he had this idea that if anything strange or disruptive was going on, young Alex Debogorski probably knew something about it.

Oh, I've got so many bear stories, I don't know where to put them all. One time Fred Doll and I come off a night shift at the McIntyre Porcupine Mine and we decide to go for a little drive. I've always been a big fan of hitting the road on a moment's notice—you just gas up the vehicle and go. On more than one occasion I've gone for a drive around the block and phoned my wife from 800 miles away. She's pretty patient about that sort of thing. No matter what is going on in your life, it always puts a new perspective on things once you see that big, wide-open road.

So anyway, that's what Fred and I do. We gas her up and head south. It's a summer day, 1975, and we pick up a case of beer and head for Banff National Park. Beautiful big mountains, green forests, rushing rivers. We've got the windows rolled down and we're having a great time. Sometimes in the park you will see tourists pulled up at the side of the road, looking at animals, so when we see a car stopped, I say to Fred, "Let's pull over and see what they're looking at."

It was a big Buick station wagon with California plates, and this elderly couple was looking at a bear. Fred pulls over on the wrong side of the road, stops, rolls down his window, and this mother bear with a little cub comes walking over to the car. The mother bear stands up and puts her paws on the door and sticks her head right inside the window. Fred is just about smelling her armpit she's so far inside the window, and I decide that this will make an excellent picture if I take it from outside. So I say, "Fred, hold on to the bear so she can't pull her head out, and I'll sneak outside and take a photo."

I grab the disposable camera off the dashboard and climb out of the car and hurry around the other side to capture this bear half inside the window of Fred's Torino. Well, I guess Fred didn't want to grab the bear by the head, because as soon as I come up behind her and the cub she pulls her head out of the window and hisses and comes after me. I had never heard a bear make that sound before, but she hisses just like a cat. I scuttle back around to my side of the car, keeping my rear end toward the bear, figuring at any moment she's going to bite my behind because that's where her nose is. But I manage to jump back in the car and slam the door without injury, and Fred doesn't tease me about being scared of the bear. No matter how big and tough you think you are, the sight of a bear coming at you will get you moving.

So now the old couple from California are just shaking their heads at the foolishness of what I just did. The mother bear lies down in the ditch with her cub, right next to their big Buick wagon, and they start taking pictures of her. Now I get a new idea. "Fred, go down there and stand beside the bear and I'll take a picture of you, the momma bear, and the bear cub.

You kind of look like a bear anyway, and we could mail it off to people as your family portrait."

Fred decides that this is a good idea, so he gets out of the car and saunters down into the ditch and comes up behind the bear. She's not paying any attention to him, so I go over to the Buick and get the camera all ready, and when he's right behind her, he's not sure how to make her stand up for the photo, so he reaches down and taps her on the shoulder.

Well, she gives an enormous roar and comes off the ground like she's been launched by a spring. She wheels around and comes after Fred like she's going to tear him apart, and even though he's about twenty-five feet from the old couple's Buick I swear he makes it to the front hood of their car in one big leap. Boom, he lands butt-first on the hood with his legs cocked back and his boots aimed right at the bear. I snap the photograph just as the bear's nose is almost touching his boot. In the picture, it looks like the bear is about to sniff his boot heel. One second later, he kicks her hard in the nose, and she thinks better of attacking him, drops to the ground, rounds up her cub, and off she goes.

We climb into our car and drive away, leaving that poor old couple from California staring at the dent in their hood. They probably went home and told all their friends about these two crazy Canadians who got chased by a bear and ended up on the hood of their car.

My Number Comes Up

I knew that sooner or later I was going to get it, but when my number came up I wasn't even on the mountain.

One day in 1975 I'm clearing the mud away from the front of the shop at the top of the mountain at Number 9 Mine in

Grande Cache with a CAT-12 grader. I'm backing up for another pass when this guy in a sixty-five-ton Terex rock truck backs out of the garage. A driver is supposed to look back and blow the horn twice before you back up, and I maintain to this day that he didn't do that. And here he comes out of the garage and backs right into me. The sloping back on the rock box comes up onto the cab of the grader and starts crushing it on top of me. My left leg snaps. You talk about going into shock—well, it's just like my head is filling up with foam. I'm holding on to the wheel and the whole cab is crumbling. The interior of the cab has a rollover protection system—a big cage of steel bars—and as that monster truck keeps coming, the bars are groaning and the glass is popping out of the windshield. Very slowly the cab starts to fold forward and I'm sitting there holding the wheel, in shock, thinking to myself that I'm probably going to die, and wondering how long it's going to be before my life starts flashing before my eyes.

Just as my chest starts pressing up against the steering wheel the engine of the rock truck stalls. The back window is popped out and I'm tilted forward with my chest against the wheel getting ready to die, and all movement suddenly ceases. All of this takes place in a couple of seconds, of course. The rock truck moves ahead and this big Irish mechanic and some other guys come running, trying to get me out. Because of the shock I can't really talk. I can just barely croak. And these guys take hold of me. They have their hands underneath my arms and they start bouncing me, back and forth and up and down, and I'm trying to tell them, "Just lift me straight up! Do it nice and slow! And I'll slide out from under the steering wheel!"

But of course I'm just croaking, barely audible, and they can't hear me. Finally they give up and just leave me draped over the steering wheel. The seat is tilted forward from the collision and the vinyl is slippery, so I keep sliding down and I'm trying to hold myself up with my right leg, which is all the support I have because my left leg is broken and it hurts like heck. So they call the shovel mechanic and he comes roaring up in the service truck and I'm leaning over the steering wheel getting ready to faint from the pain in my leg. One of the guys jumps into the grader and lights the cutting torch. He's going to cut the steering column. He lights the torch and about two feet of flame pop out of that torch right in front of my eyes and burn off my whiskers. I look through the flame and I can see all that diesel fuel on the floor.

Right away, I see this vision of myself burning to death, and wow, I jump like a squirrel. I grab the roof of that cab and I'm out of there in a split second. As soon I'm out of the crushed cab it's like a hundred tons of pressure come off me. By this time the ambulance has arrived. It backs up to the grader and the door flies open and six or eight men come at me. I'm up on the grader saying, "It's okay, I'll jump down!"

I'm hopping on one leg, climbing down, and those guys grab me and literally throw me into the ambulance. The ambulance is spinning its wheels and throwing gravel, and as we go roaring out of the yard, two guys are running behind it, trying to close its doors. I look up and there's this beautiful nurse leaning over me. I don't know where they found her, but anyway she's a vision of loveliness and for a moment or two I have this uneasy feeling that I've actually died in between the wreck and the ambulance and now this angel is taking me up to heaven.

I didn't find out until later, but apparently I started taking off my clothes. She says to me, "What are you doing?"

"Don't you want me to take my clothes off?"

She says, "No, you can leave your coveralls on. I can put on the air splint over your pants."

I don't know how my buddies found out about any of this, but weeks later they had a good time bugging me about it—here's Alex with a broken leg and he's trying to make time in the ambulance with the nurse.

So we go roaring down the mountain, heading for the hospital. I guess the drivers figure that if I didn't get killed in the wreckage they might as well try and kill me on the way down the hill. This is our rough, miserable road and these ambulances have truck suspension, and I'm telling you we're hitting some of these holes so hard that I swear they almost broke my other leg during that thirty-mile drive. We get to the hospital and they rush me in the door. "We need to give you some Demerol," says the doctor.

"Well, you better call my wife first," I say, because I know that as soon as they give me that needle I'm going to be out like a light. Sure enough, right after I talk to Louise they hit me up with Demerol and I can't remember a single thing for the week that followed.

My brother Richie had been drinking a little bit, worried about my situation, and he was real upset that the doctor in charge of my case didn't want to send me to the big hospital down in Edmonton. These little small-town hospitals have to deal with a lot of serious injuries, construction workers and rig hands and so on, so I guess they figured if he's going to die he is going to die, that's nothing unusual. He's just a coal miner, and there's lots more where he came from. Richie took a different point of view. He wanted them to pull out all the stops and fly me by air ambulance to a real hospital in Edmonton.

Finally he decided that if the doctors wouldn't fly me out, he would. There was a little twin-engine airplane sitting on the grass at the local airstrip and Richie found a pilot who said he knew how to fly it. I guess it's not that hard to steal an airplane, at least in those days it wasn't, and Richie's plan was that he was going to check me out of the hospital, steal this airplane, load me into it, and fly me to Edmonton. Of course, the doctor didn't want to check me out because I was in such bad shape. Then Richie said he was gonna kill the doctor and that caused a bit of a kerfuffle.

Richie had this idea in his mind that he and his buddy would steal the plane, then once we arrived in Edmonton, he would give the pilot a chance to get away, and then he would phone the ambulance. If the cops arrived he would tell them that he stole the airplane himself. Richie couldn't fly a plane, but he figured the cops didn't have to know that. So this was his master plan, but just when he was ready to set the wheels in motion my medical condition went from bad to worse.

A little piece of fat traveled up my leg from the site of the injury and ended up in my right lung and gave me an embolism. My lung collapsed. The long and short of it was, I was way too sick to get hijacked out of the hospital, and it was just as well because the trip to Edmonton probably would've killed me, and that would have been the end of another one of Richie's smart ideas.

Louise came to visit. As per usual, I would start a sentence, doze off from the Demerol, wake up, and try to complete the same sentence. Quite often I didn't make a lot of sense. After one particular sentence, I dozed off but didn't come back to finish it. As Louise was waiting, she was looking me over and noticed my toes and fingers were turning blue. She called the nurse. I had gotten a case of hospital pneumonia and my temperature was 105 degrees.

The nurse brought a tub full of crushed ice and water and stuck it beside the bed and she and Louise would dip a blanket in that ice water, get it freezing cold, and then throw it on top of me. Holy smokes, when that ice-cold blanket hit me it was like getting electrocuted. I would let out a big roar, but I was so weak and hoarse that the roar would come out like a squeaky blast of air. When they pulled that icy blanket off me I just felt like I was floating on a cloud. Then they would dip it in the tub and get it all crusted up with ice again and throw it on top of me, and boy, that was like torture.

Finally, Louise and the nurse managed to get my body temperature down with those ice blankets and I avoided brain damage. Well, some people might argue with that, but the doctors said that I came pretty close to dying or suffering permanent disability. After about ten days I came back from the brink and started feeling better, and of course I then began to disrupt the hospital pretty good.

Louise was coming to visit me and it occurred to me that we hadn't had sex for quite a while. The nurse was in the room, and I said to her, "I'd like to have sex with my wife when she comes to visit."

The nurse said, "Alex, you can't do that, it's against the rules."

"Why? We're adults, we have a marriage certificate. You never know, I could be dead next week. It might be my last chance to make love with my wife. Why can't you just close the door and leave us alone for a while?"

I guess the nurse thought I was kidding, because she dropped the subject. When Louise came to visit, I said, "Why don't you climb up into this bed with me and draw the curtain?"

You know what it's like when you're in the hospital, everybody's trying to be nice to you, so Louise climbs up into the bed and the next thing you know she's got her pants off. Well, the nurse hears all the suspicious rustling going on behind the curtain and I can hear her boots squeaking off down the hallway as she heads for the nursing station. Next thing you know it sounds like a flock of chickens are erupting down the hall. There is an outburst of squawking and clucking and you can just hear the whole works of them coming with the matron at the head of a flock. This old head nurse bursts into the room with all her assistants behind her and she rips back the curtain, pulls back the sheets, and pulls Louise out of my bed.

There's Louise with her pants around her ankles, completely embarrassed, and me with a body cast up to my waist and we're doing our best to make a little whoopee in a hospital bed. I immediately close one eye and pretend to be half dead. It was hilarious, but not for Louise. The head nurse is not impressed.

"Mrs. Debogorski!" she squawks. "This man is half dead! Have you no common sense?"

What the heck's the problem? I thought. *We're in a hospital. If nothing else, I appreciated the entertainment!*

Anyway, we survived it. Got out of the hospital after two weeks, had to go to Edmonton to get rehabilitation for my leg. That led to more adventures. I was limping around the town on my bad leg and decided I might as well go for a drink at the Kingsway bar. If you went to the Kingsway bar you were always pretty sure you would see somebody you knew. There were always about five hundred people in there, and if you didn't know anyone you could make a friend pretty quickly. That was one rough place. The bikers and the paratroopers would have a few drinks and then go at one another, providing lots of entertainment for the spectators, and people got killed in there on a pretty regular basis.

So I was sitting in there having a drink with a couple of people I knew, and this kerfuffle started. Some guy was waving a knife around and the hotel staff threw him out. Good riddance. I've never had much patience with these chicken-shit guys who pull out a knife when trouble starts. If you can't defend yourself with your fists, then stay home.

A little while later I left the bar and this troublemaker was standing over on the other side of the street with a knife in his hand. Some people from the bar were yelling at him, but nobody had the nerve to go over and mix it up with him because he had this knife in his hand. I can't remember if it was a big knife or a little knife, but it doesn't really matter, because you can poke somebody in the chest with a little butter knife and kill them.

After everybody lost interest in yelling at this guy and went back into the bar, I propped myself up against a piece of broken concrete to rest my injured leg and yelled at him, "Hey, city boy! Why don't you come on over here and have a little talk with this country boy?"

I was baiting him, trying to make him mad enough to cross the street. My plan was, I was going to take that knife away and give him a licking. So I stood there for about ten minutes, teasing him and daring him to walk across the street. But he wouldn't come, so I lost interest and went into the bar.

Next thing you know the cops pulled up. I could see the red lights flipping through the window, so I went back outside and crossed the street to see if this guy had pointy ears and sharp teeth or what.

This cop had him in handcuffs up against the side of the police car. The cop was head and shoulders taller than the kid with a knife, and you could see that the cop was so mad his eyes were practically glowing in the dark. As I walked past, the kid looked at me and said, "What have you got to say for yourself now, asshole?"

Well, I just had an airlock right there. I couldn't even move. I wound up and gave that kid such a backhand that his head whipped right around. The cop was so shocked that he lifted the kid up right off the ground by his handcuffed wrists.

The cop yelled at me, "You're under arrest for assault and battery! Go and stand over there!"

"Where?"

"Over there!"

"Yes, sir."

I was all obedient with this cop. Never argue with someone who has a gun, especially if he's wearing a uniform. The cop threw the kid in the back of the car, and after a few minutes he came over to see me. "The kid doesn't want to press charges," he said.

"Thank you, sir."

So he let me go. I can just imagine why the kid decided not to press charges—the cop probably told him that he was putting us in the same cell.

Anyway, that's the story of my broken leg and my rehabilitation. Once you hurt yourself you're never a hundred percent afterward, and that lung embolism followed me around my whole life. During the second season of *Ice Road Truckers*, I was up in Inuvik, on the Arctic coast, when I got short of breath. I would get out of the truck to do my normal chores and right away I would have this tight feeling in my chest, almost like I had eaten too much, and I would feel short of breath. I was coughing blood, too. I went to the hospital and they ran a few tests and said I seemed okay. But this young doctor was concerned and she insisted that I go to Yellowknife and have more tests. So I went over there and had a CT scan, which showed that one lung had a clot and my heart was beating way too fast. They kept me in the hospital and thinned out my blood and put me on medication to prevent more clots. It took months before I felt normal again. While the doctors were treating me they asked me about my health history and I told them about the fatty embolism and the collapsed lung that happened after that guy backed into me. They said once you have a clot in the vicinity of your lung it can happen again at any time.

So I'm still dealing with that accident over thirty years later. And it never would have happened if that truck driver had looked in his rearview mirror.

Go North, Young Man

Like most things in life, I more or less ended up going north by accident—and I mean by accident. In 1975, while I was recovering in the hospital from getting crushed by that rock truck, I met a fellow who was in there being treated for silicosis and he started telling me stories about gold prospecting. Well, that got me excited. If there's one subject that can get a young man feeling all twitchy, it's gold.

I grew up listening to that song "North to Alaska" and dreaming of the gold rush—men driving sled dogs across frozen lakes, panning for gold, and celebrating in some honky-tonk saloon after they'd hit pay dirt. At one point I even went to the geology department at the University of Alberta to see if I could find a geologist who could tell me where to go looking for gold. I ended up getting an interview with this guy named Professor Dalton, who told me, "Son, the place to go looking for gold is Yellowknife. Read some books on the subject. Get a hammer and a magnifying glass. Drive up to Yellowknife. Park your car, walk back into the bush as far as you can walk, start breaking rocks, and you'll find gold. I did my field studies there during the Second World War, and there is visible gold all over the place."

So anyway, now I'm in the hospital and this guy is telling me there's big money to be made in gold prospecting. And you don't have to go all the way up north! British Columbia has plenty of gold, and all it takes is some young man with a pair of boots and a sleeping bag who's got the gumption to hike off into the bush and claim it.

This fellow is older and more experienced than me. (He must have been forty years old, and I was twenty-two, which made him an old-timer in my eyes.) So I figure I have something to learn from him. He offers to make me his partner and we shake hands on it. As soon as we're out of the hospital I quit my job and head off to Barkerville, B.C., with my new partner. I'm driving a brand-new four-wheel-drive Ford pickup with a sleek two-tone paint job and nice wheels and deluxe upholstery and I couldn't be happier. No more slugging it out on some job site. Barkerville is where the Cariboo Gold Rush got started, and it's like a place from an old movie—rugged country, wild rivers, and lots of stories of men who took the big gamble and made a fortune.

Well, of course, if gold were easy to find, it wouldn't be so valuable. After looking the country over, talking to the locals, and doing some research at the government geological office in Quesnel, I staked a claim. My partner, Jean-Guy, didn't like getting his hands dirty. He liked to do "research." The claim I staked was the old Starleta claim. It had been part of a stock market play sometime before.

We're camping out, getting dirty, eating bad food, breaking rocks, and finding very little gold. Finally, after two months of this, I'm dead broke and just about starving to death. Ford Motor Credit is looking for me because I'm driving their brand-new pickup and I haven't made any payments on it for three months. Shell Oil is real interested in finding out where I am so they can get their credit card back. Meanwhile, my wife is very unhappy because I've vanished to go off looking for gold and she has no money to feed our children, Shielo and Curtis, who are about four and two at this point. She's called upon her dad for help, and he's driven up to Grand Cache in his grain truck and rescued her and taken her back to Fairview, where she's now living in this little apartment and relying on the support of her family. All in all, it's a bust, and I'm beginning to learn what thousands of young prospectors have learned before me—the main thing you find when you go gold prospecting is poverty.

So it's off to Fairview to rejoin my wife. She's happy to see me, and we get along fine for a week or two, and then of course the happiness wears off and we both agree that I need to get a real job. Enough of this gold-prospecting bullshit. She's always been very patient with me, but there's a time to dream and a time to make money, and we were flat broke. I didn't have any excuses, either. In those days there were jobs all over the place. Anyone who wanted work could get work in a day or two. So it wasn't a question of finding any old job as much as figuring out the best job and the best place to go. Some time before that I had met this girl named Teresa Murphy, my sister's college friend. She said to me, "If you ever need a job and you want to come to a place that's really great, come to Yellowknife."

She was the second person who'd told me about Yellowknife. First it was the professor, who told me it was a great place to look for gold, and now it was this Teresa, telling me there was lots of work and it was a fun place to live. So I call Teresa and tell her the situation. "If you can get me a job I will come up to Yellowknife, otherwise I'm going south, down to Fox Creek, Alberta, to work in the oil fields."

Teresa says she'll make some inquiries, and asks me to call her back in a few days.

I wait for a few days, but Teresa hasn't called me back with news about Yellowknife because we don't even have a phone. I pack up my truck, load my two dogs in the cab, kiss my wife and babies good-bye, then head off to this little village called Blue Sky, Alberta, where there's a pay phone beside the road. I pop some coins in the slot and get Teresa Murphy on the phone. She says, "My dad found you a job at a place called Robinson Trucking."

"Thank you very much, Teresa. I will see you Monday morning."

So I hang up the phone and climb back into my truck and turn north instead of south, driving to Yellowknife, not knowing that I would be spending the rest of my life there.

It's the beginning of August 1976, and the road to Yellowknife is nowhere near as smooth as it is now. As I drive north the pavement turns to gravel, and the gravel finally turns to mud, and then the mud road gets so bad that I'm having a hard time getting through the ruts even in my four-wheel-drive truck. To top it off, there's no place to buy gas, and I haven't brought along jerry cans of extra fuel. When I get to Edzo, about sixty miles from Yellowknife, the truck's gas tank is dead empty, but somehow the engine keeps running and I manage to carry on to Yellowknife.

I'm a bit overdue because of the road, but when I phone Teresa she says, "No problem, just go to Robinson tomorrow and you'll have a job." I don't have any money for a room, so I go out to Long Lake campground and set up my tent. On Tuesday I leave the dogs at the camp and go out to Robinson Trucking to start my job with them, running a CAT and driving a truck. They have lots of work for me. The government is moving the capital of the Northwest Territories from Fort Smith to Yellowknife. There are two large operating gold mines right in the city, and everything is going great guns. If you can saw a board in half, you've got a job. Can you start tomorrow? Great, you're hired. If you weren't a drunk you had it made. And if you were a drunk, you probably had a job anyway. Guys would walk up to you and say, "Nail down that floor and I'll pay you two hundred dollars."

The place is full of women, too. Nice-looking young women. This was a shock to me, coming from backwoods Alberta. You'd go to a dance back home and there wouldn't be a woman in sight who wasn't taken. You'd end up dancing with a coat rack. Yellowknife, the capital city and a government center, was full of secretaries and waitresses and office girls. I learned a little lesson, and if I was talking to a young man today I would say, "If you're looking for a wife, go to Yellowknife." Of course, I had a wife already, so I wasn't in the market, but I still noticed all these women walking around.

My plan is to dig myself out of debt, but it's dicey because Ford Motor Credit is still looking for their brand-new pickup truck, and Shell is looking for their credit card. If either of them catch up with me, I'll lose my transportation and my job, too. So I need to elude them until I've earned enough money to get current with my payments. In those days if you bought less than fifty dollars with your charge card they wouldn't phone it in, so I make sure to keep my purchases under fifty dollars and meanwhile I'm living like a hunted outlaw.

Teresa, the girl who's gotten me the job, is working at the hospital in the kitchen and that's how I get food. I tell her I have these two dogs and would appreciate any scraps for them. She says, "No problem, there's lots of garbage from the hospital kitchen."

For the next couple of weeks that's how I stay alive. Every few days Teresa fills a couple of plastic bags with scraps, thinking it's for the dogs, and that's how the dogs and I survive.

Every night at six o'clock I get off work, filthy and tired, and go home to Long Lake. They have a wooden raft a hundred feet offshore, and I swim out there with a little piece of soap in my pocket and hide behind the raft and scrub myself off.

The other swimmers are giving me funny looks because I'm treading water, acting natural, and there's this big cloud of soap bubbles rising all around me. Washing in the lake works pretty well until autumn comes, but with the arrival of the cold weather at least there's no one around to watch me lather up. My last swim in Long Lake takes place on October 6, and it's so cold that when I plunge into the water I'm almost paralyzed, and there are black spots twirling in front of my eyes as I gallop back ashore!

Eventually, after about a month, the Parks people kick me out of the campground, so I set up my tent in the equipment yard at Robinson Trucking. I had to move again when Robinson's decided to build their new shop right where my tent was pitched. Just when it looked like things can't get much worse, I met a salesman who worked for Bowman Bolts. His name was Greg Dexter. He invited me to share his apartment at Rockridge with him. It was none too soon because it was colder than heck and winter was coming. After I had lived with him for a couple of months, I found out he was an uncle of one of my buddies from Grande Cache.

Ernie Filowich gave me his taxi, car 6, to drive, so I no longer needed the vehicle. I sold my truck and used the money to pay off Ford Motor Credit. Robinson's did a fall lay-off and I was part of it. That October I started my own business, Eagle North Contracting. Pretty soon I was working day and night. By day I was contracting and by night I was driving the taxi and working as a bouncer at the Explorer Hotel in a cabaret called the Snowshoe.

4

LIFE IS A CABARET

"Can't dance, can't sing, but boy, I've got a
hard head. Punch me and you're going to
hurt your hand."

My job is to check identification at the door, make sure
no one comes in with a knife or other weapon, keep the
place under control, and take the cover charge. Yellowknife is
a pretty wild community, and this is the best party bar in the
town, so it's an intense job. You've got a couple hundred people in the room, and when the party gets going there's always
some guy who starts causing trouble. In an emergency you've
got the bartender and the waiters for backup, but they're not
getting paid to do your job, so 99 percent of the time you're
pretty much on your own.

But I've been fighting drunks all my life, so I figure I might
as well get paid for it. Plus I got my liquor for free.

High Noon at the Snowshoe Bar

Most of the time I bounced by myself. Of course, you had the waiters and the bartender to help you out occasionally, but I usually depended on customers when the fights got too big and they would jump in and give me a hand. Sometimes you'd get in a fight and you'd be fairly confident that you weren't going to have too much of a problem, but when a fight starts, strange things can happen.

I remember one night about eight o'clock, the band hadn't started yet and there weren't very many customers. I was about twenty-three years old, and this young fellow started trouble. I was smoking a long cigarillo-type thing called a More. I punched this fellow and knocked him back a bit, and just as he was coming at me I tapped the ash off the cigarette, put it back in my mouth, and let him have it right between the eyes. I didn't hurt him any. Hurt his dignity, I guess you could say, but the whole point was trying to look cool. Those Clint Eastwood spaghetti Westerns were popular at that time and everyone was doing their best to look cool.

Our impaired clients presented plenty of challenges, but every once in a while a guy will come in, stone sober, and take you on. That happened to me more than once. I remember this one guy who came in. I'd never seen him before, but he just lit into me for no reason. I had the chain up at the door and a two-dollar cover charge, and he just ranted and raved and called me everything in the book. Even after he sat down he wouldn't shut up. I had a couple of customers come up and ask me why I wouldn't slap him because they were getting kind of fed up with the way he was carrying on. I told them it was okay and I just ignored him.

But he wouldn't stop, and one thing led to another, and he finally gave me a cuff or something. I grabbed him and drove him down a little flight of stairs, and I ended up kneeling on top of him with my hands raised getting ready to hit him just on the side of the head. I figured I would stun him, stand him up, shove him outside, and hold the door shut until he got tired of wrestling with the door handle and went home.

Then he whispered something.

I said, "Pardon me?"

When you're fighting you kind of get that roaring in your head, and I missed what he said. I went to hit him again and he whispered something again.

"Pardon me?"

He was talking really softly, and after all the yelling and screaming I couldn't believe my ears.

He says, "Boy, you have a lot of patience."

I'm kneeling on top of him. "Excuse me?"

"Boy, you have a lot of patience."

"Are you going to be okay?"

"Yeah."

"Can I let you stand up? Or do I need to smack you again?"

"Oh, no, I'll be fine."

I'm kneeling on him and he's talking to me like we're having a cup of tea or something, and this after half an hour of verbal abuse. So I stood up, carefully, thinking that now I've let him up he's going to hit me and we're going at it again.

He shook my hand. It was almost like some kind of a test. I had this funny feeling that he was a policeman, checking to see if I could control my temper, but I don't know. Nobody had ever seen this guy and he never came back.

Other guys, you'll throw them out and they'll just go nuts. I've seen guys beat the hell out of a phone booth or punch a cement wall with their fists. It's an awful thing to watch. You're thinking, *Why isn't he punching me instead of the wall?* He's hurting himself seriously, breaking his knuckles, and not just for a night but for life.

Another night this guy came into the bar. He wasn't that big, but he had quite a reputation for being ridiculously strong. He worked in the mine and they called him the Buffalo. It was early in the evening. The band wasn't playing yet. Nobody was drunk and there was hardly anybody in the bar. Then the Buffalo walked in with his buddies, and without saying a word he walked up to me and gave me a slap across the face.

So of course the fight was on. I hit him in the solar plexus and I thought, *Holy mackerel, the guy is like a rock.* I was only twenty-three and I didn't know that God made people that hard. I hit him three times in the chest area as hard as I could and he didn't even flinch. I thought, *Uh-oh, this is not working.* Finally I kind of curled my fist and caught him just on the point of the chin under the ear. This wasn't a hard punch compared to the others. I just tapped him there and he dropped like a bag of sand. After a moment or two he climbed up off the floor and put out his hand. "Thank you," he said. "That's enough for me."

"Are you sure?"

"Yes, sir, have a good night."

He nodded to his friends and they all walked out the door.

Well, I didn't know it at the time, but they were testing me. It happened fairly regularly and I never caught on. It was thirty years before I found out. Some of the guys I fought with became my friends later. And about five years ago, I mentioned it to some of them and they burst out laughing. They said, "You were new in town. You weren't a northerner, so we thought we'd have some fun."

They explained that they'd find a big guy who was pretty tough, buy him a bunch of drinks, bet some money, and dare him to come in and fight me. By the end of the night he'd be all primed up and ready to come over to the Snowshoe and give me a beating. He'd walk in and give me a cuff in the nose and the fight would be on. I'd knock him down to his knees or whatever and the guy would get up and say, "Thank you very much. Have a good evening."

And he'd shake my hand and I'd think, *Thank me for what?* Are these people mad at themselves? Why is he thanking me for knocking him on his ass? I never clued in that it was a setup. There's only so much entertainment in a mining town, and these guys were laughing when they told me about it. "Oh, heck, we just wanted to see how tough you were."

Here Come the Cops

I've always gotten along with the police. In fact, I came very close to becoming a cop myself. When I was a young guy, I was pretty much torn between police work and becoming a soldier. My dad, having been in the military for twelve years, taught me respect for anyone in uniform. It may have bothered a lot of Canadians, but I wanted to join the U.S. military and go to Vietnam, largely because of the anti-Communist leanings in my family. Many of my relatives had been put in Siberia by the Communists and as a result some died. So like a lot of young men everywhere, I wanted to find adventure and go over to the jungles of Southeast Asia and fight communism on the side of the good guys.

My second choice would have been police work. I thought of policing as a sort of civilian version of the military—you're out doing battle with the bad guys every day. I could see myself getting a lot of satisfaction from that. I didn't mind conflict. However, I ended up moving north and becoming a jack-of–all-trades and an ice road trucker. But whenever I see a guy in a police car I think, *That could be me.*

I didn't like calling in the police for backup when I was working as a bouncer. They've got their own problems to deal with, and if it wasn't a real emergency I would try to handle it on my own. You can't use excessive force and you have to be reasonable, but if the cops get to know you and come to understand that you are a responsible person, they let you handle the drunks with whatever force is required. And frankly, I would be happy to return the favor. More than once, I've helped cops who were having a hard time arresting somebody.

Cops are better educated, but they aren't as big as they used to be. I've got nothing against higher education, but there is nothing better for defusing a potentially violent situation than a couple of guys weighing a quarter of a ton between them showing up at somebody's door. I mean, when I call a cop, I want to see a cop, not some soft-spoken guy with an ear stud and a degree in political correctness. You might think that I'm arguing for the good old days when cops could be violent with no repercussions, but I'm saying the opposite. It was very rare to hear of a cop shooting anybody in the old days. They kept their guns tucked away in a holster with a leather flap over it. If you lipped one off, he would knock you on your ass. If you pulled a knife, he'd break your arm with a nightstick.

The trouble with these sensitive New Age cops is that they're too quick to shoot somebody when they feel threatened. They're not physically confident. They're afraid of getting overpowered by some guy who's a lot bigger than them, so that's when they pull out the pepper spray, the Taser, or the gun. I don't know how many times I've seen the news clips on television. Some guy walks toward the cops with a screwdriver or a knife, and what do they do? They shoot him! It makes me crazy! I mean, I would take that weapon away from that guy in two seconds.

I could do it easily because I've handled hundreds of violent people·working as a bouncer. The trouble is, these young cops have too little training in fighting. If you walk up to a fearful dog, his fear is going to make him aggressive. It's the same with a fearful cop. If some citizen gets out of control because he's been drinking or taking drugs, he'd better show deference to the police who show up to deal with him. But he's not going to show deference to them, because he's out of his mind. He's going to attack them, and they are going to Taser him or shoot him because they are afraid of violent people.

The bottom line is, a fearful police officer is a dangerous police officer. They teach these young cops to get out their gun and shoot to kill if they fear that their life is in danger. Well, who decides if their life is in danger? It's all subjective. If someone starts walking toward you with a pair of scissors in his hand or a knife, is that a good reason to kill that person? With any kind of training at all you can easily disarm a guy like that with your bare hands, if you know what you're doing. If you have a nightstick in your hands it's like taking candy from a baby.

I often talk to the retired Royal Canadian Mounted Police who work on security in the diamond mines. These are the old guys from the old days. All these guys are six-two, they're all big men, and they don't think much of the new RCMP. They think that policing has really gone downhill. This one old RCMP guy told me he always carried a baseball bat behind the seat of his cruiser car. He also carried a glove and a baseball under the seat of the car, and when things got quiet he would hit a few pop flies for the neighborhood kids. He practiced what you call neighborhood policing before all those sociologists announced that they invented it. He knew all the kids by name, and he knew which ones needed a pat on the back and which ones needed a kick in the ass.

He told me once that he pulled up to arrest these three hooligans. There's three of them and one of him. And these are big, tough guys with criminal records. These guys are leaning against a fence and as soon as he gets out of his car they nudge one another and start laughing at him. And so he opens the back door and slips that baseball bat up against his leg and walks up to them. He's not making a big show out of it, he's just strolling up to them with that baseball bat.

And their smiles kind of fade away as he taps that Slugger against his leg and tells them to get in the car. So they look at one another, and nobody says anything. None of them are smiling anymore. Nobody wants to be the first one to challenge this cop and get whacked on the thigh with a hickory bat. So they walk to that police car and climb in the backseat. End of problem. Nowadays, you would need a team of cops and three or four cruisers to pick those guys up. The strobe lights would be flashing and they would be putting on a big show for the neighborhood. But this old boy didn't need emergency lights and he didn't need backup. And he didn't need his pistol. All he needed was a persuader and the knowledge that he could handle this situation. The sad thing is, if he was on the job today and threatened three upstanding citizens like these with a baseball bat, he would probably lose his job.

Another old cop told me he used to have to deal with violent people suffering from schizophrenia. They were potentially dangerous, to themselves and everyone around them. This one particular guy would go off his medication every once in a while and start screaming and yelling. And his family would call the RCMP, and the guy would come out of the kitchen with a knife and start ranting and raving when they arrived, saying, "Go ahead and shoot me!"

This old cop was not afraid of someone armed with a knife. He knew that he could take the knife away if it came to that. So he would talk to the man calmly. He'd say, "Hey, nice to see you, how is your brother Bob?"

"Bob? He's at work."

The guy would totally forget that he was angry. It was just like he had turned off a switch. "Okay, that's good. Say hello to Bob for me."

"Okay, Constable, I'll do that."

"Do you mind if we come in for a cuppa tea?"

"Tea? Sure, I guess. Come on in."

He'd come in and sit down at the kitchen table with this guy. The guy would still have that big butcher knife in his hand, and he'd be making tea with his other hand. A constable would say, "Now, Frankie, you haven't taken your medication, have you?"

"I don't know. I can't remember."

"Well, I'm pretty sure you haven't taken it. Would you do me a favor?"

"What's that?"

"Would you take your pills for me? Could you do it right in front of me here?"

So the guy would get out his pills and they would sit down at the table and have a cup of tea and the guy would take his pills, and after a few minutes he would look at that big knife in his hand like he couldn't remember why he was carrying it. Today, standard police training would have the cops shoot that guy the minute he waved that knife at them. It happens all the time. The other day, the police went out to this guy's house, he came down the stairs with a knife in his hand, and they put three friggin' bullets in his chest. They told him to stop a couple of times and that was it.

So that's my tirade. It seems that most of the people the police shoot aren't really criminals, just sick and in need of help.

I remember this one Friday night in 1982, I came out of the Gold Range Hotel and this RCMP officer had a girl handcuffed to the back of my pickup truck. It was an old orange CN truck with a ladder rack on it, and he had her handcuffed to the rack. I guess she had been driving drunk or some darned thing and she was giving him a hard time. I was going to stay out of this kerfuffle, so I went into the Rec Hall bar while this policeman questioned her.

When I came back out, all hell was breaking loose. He had left the police car with the door open and the engine running, and while he was behind the police car with this girl, her friends came staggering out of the bar. One of her friends said, "Oh, there's my car," and climbed into the police car.

I don't know if she realized it was a police car or not, but she just climbed in, slammed the door, threw it into reverse, and floored it. When it started spinning backward, she realized she was going the wrong way and was going to run over her friend and this cop, so she put it in drive and floored it.

She had the gas pedal pinned to the floor, holding the wheel, gritting her teeth, and I was running toward the car to stop her.

Next thing, the policeman emerged from behind the police car. He ran up to the door. Its wheels were spinning on the ice, and he had his hand on the front fender trying to stop it. Obviously he couldn't stop it that way, so he took out his gun and started shooting—*bang, bang, bang,* shooting the tire. He had the gun six inches from the tire and he was blasting away trying to disable the car before it could speed up.

Then the car took off and went by me and I thought, *Oh, no*, because it was heading right for another girl who had fallen on her ass on the road. She was lying in the middle right in its path, but the police car was fishtailing so badly that it wove into the other lane and slid right past her.

This young cop was totally overwhelmed. He stuck the gun back in its holster and the bloody gun went off just as he was putting it away. He had put five bullets into the tire and the sixth one went off and the bullet hit the road right beside his foot. Damn near shot his own foot off.

Well, I mean, this was pretty bad, you know. He's just unloaded his gun on a tire, he's got a girl handcuffed on the street and she is almost run over, and he's totally overwhelmed.

Now all these people from both bars are gathering around this policeman, screaming at him. The girl's friends are all about the same age as her, and they're all jumping all over him, scratching his face, mauling him. The crowds are cheering them on, and there must be forty or fifty people there. So I run up to the policeman. "What's your name and unit number? I'll call for help."

He's helpless. He doesn't have his radio. He doesn't even have any bullets for his gun. He's on his hands and knees holding this girl, and these other girls are jumping on him, and he looks up at me and I have never seen a more thankful-looking face in my life. He tells me his name and unit number and I run into the restaurant, where I call the police station and tell them this crowd is going to beat the hell out of one of their officers if they don't get reinforcements over here.

Right away they start asking me my name and birth date, the color of my eyes, the length of my pecker, and what have you. After a minute or so of this nonsense I say, "Look, I'm going out there to help him fight this mob, or he's not going to survive. Good-bye."

Within minutes there's policemen coming from all directions. Cop cars squealing up from all over the place, and some people I never even knew were policemen. There were guys in their pajamas, guys jumping over fences, guys in rusty old trucks. They all heard the call go out on the radio. "Officer needs assistance. Shots fired."

I didn't know these were all police people, but boy, they were coming out of the cracks, and in minutes it all got straightened out.

The funny thing was, I could not believe that the dispatcher kept me on the phone for all that time asking me stupid questions. I mean really stupid questions. A couple of days later I ended up talking to two young policemen who were out on the town and I asked them about that. They said that the cops would often play jokes on each other and phone in to the dispatcher with crank calls, so maybe the dispatcher wanted to make sure that I wasn't just another cop pulling her leg.

After that, I would be listening to the scanner in the middle of the night and I began to realize that the cops were using all these fancy numbers and codes just to kid with each other. They made it sound like they were following a major case, but in fact they were stopping by the hotel to pick up a newspaper.

The cops are joking with each other on the radio all the time, but it has a serious side to it. If one of them gets into a jam, the other guys will show up in a jiffy and swarm anyone who puts up resistance. It's safety in numbers.

In the old days the Texas Rangers had a slogan that expressed their philosophy of policing: "One riot, one Ranger."

Those days are gone.

On the other hand, these police officers do look after our well-being and should have our individual support, through

My dad, Stanley Debogorski, in Sabratha, Libya, when he fought with the British Army in 1949, the year the UN General Assembly voted that Libya should become an independent state.

My mum, Irene Debogorski, holding me at the farm north of Berwyn, Alberta, in the winter of 1953.

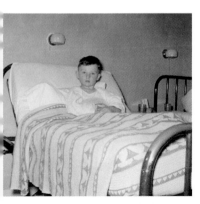

Me at the Berwyn hospital when I was six, recovering from a broken leg after a truck accident while driving with Dad.

Our family portrait from 1966. Left to right: Mark, Richard, Dad, Simone, and me.

Me with a 303 Lee Enfield rifle after bringing home a black bear from a successful hunt in 1967. I sold that bear to my longtime family friend, Fats Newton.

My tenth-grade school picture from Lloyd Garrison High School in Berwyn, Alberta, 1968.

Me and my brother Richie at the family farm north of Berwyn, Alberta, 1969.

Me and Louise on our wedding day, January 28, 1972. Standing beside us are (left to right) Louise's brother Doug, sister Betty, cousin Judy Doll, my best man Lloyd Paul, my sister Simone, and Louise's brother Leo.

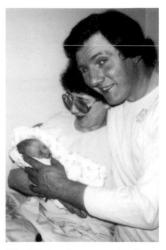

The birth of our son Andrew at the Stanton Hospital in Yellowknife on February 27, 1986.

Holding our son Curtis, with daughter Shielo, in Grande Cache, Alberta, 1975.

Talking to our son Ezekiel in Yellowknife, August 1994.

Standing in front of a hundred-ton Electra Haul coal truck at McIntyre Porcupine Coal Mine in Grande Cache, Alberta, 1974. This is the same type of truck in which a gal missed a shift and fought the truck all the way down to her death.

Riding with my daughter Shielo in City Cab #6 in front of our first mobile home in Yellowknife, 1977.

After heart surgery with my wife Louise and son Ezekiel in the chapel of the Yellowknife Stanton Hospital, 2001. The injury I sustained from the Terex rock truck in 1975 continues to haunt me.

The caterpillar 12 grader I was driving when hit by a 65-ton Terex rock truck in Grande Cache, Alberta, 1975.

Checking out my 1969 IHC Fleetstar 2000 dump truck after being forced off the road by a car in July 1985. Just one of many trucks in my company, Eagle North Contracting.

In my 1981 Western Star tractor. I used this photo for my campaign for Mayor of Yellowknife in 1994.

Figah eketehtso neshi
VOTE FOR ALEX
Mayor

An election sign on a car hood in both English and in North Slavey (Fort Good Hope dialect) during my mayoral campaign in 1994.

Pregame locker room shenanigans between me and my team mates of the Yellowknife Ravens All Star Broomball team prior to the start of the 1994 territorial championship game in Fort Smith. Left to right: Ronnie Payne, Jeff Pottinger, Warrick Sheppard, me, Duane Melchert, and Jason.

Family portrait at Alex Jr.'s wedding, July 8, 2006. Left to right: Dominic, Shielo, Julaine, Gianna, Andrew, grandson Logan, Nelson, Amelia, Benjamin, Alex Jr., Louise, me, Curtis, and Ezekiel.

Camping with my four eldest sons at Little Doctor Lake in the Nahanni mountains of the Northwest Territories. Left to right: Alex Jr., me, Nelson, Curtis and Andrew. Our good family friend, Lynn Fowler, offered his cabin on the lake for us to enjoy. The gun over the shoulder of Alex Jr. was the very gun I recovered after the canoe tipped while traveling across the lake.

Our family portrait at Christmas 2009. Left to right: Ezekiel, Shielo, Nelson, Amelia, Julaine, Louise, Benjamin, me, Andrew, Gianna, Curtis, Alex Jr., and Dominic.

Looking through the cracked windshield of a Kenworth tractor going to Lupin Mine on Contwoyto Lake, 357 miles north of Yellowknife in the winter of 1985.

A Crane and Gin pole truck lifting a Western Star tractor through the ice from 60 feet of water in the winter of 1990. Amazingly, the driver survived!

A Western Star truck that was hauling cement (pictured in adjacent picture) resting on the bottom of Contwoyto Lake north of Yellowknife. The dive hole is visible to the right of the truck.

thick and thin. Any weakness in the system is not their fault. It is, in fact, the fault of the federal government and their preoccupation with political correctness.

What I Learned about Fighting

Lesson one from all the professionals: Avoid fighting if you can.

Experienced fighters don't tend to fight. They're reasonable. They don't fly off the handle. If a man is experienced and knows how to fight, he feels comfortable and confident and capable of handling most situations. He'll probably talk, and say, "Look, I don't want to fight with you because we'll hurt our hands and our faces and potentially get in trouble with the law." So if you're dealing with someone who's keen to start something, it's a good sign that the guy doesn't know how to fight.

The more fighting one's been in, especially sober, you're going to be better at reading the situation and the guy you're up against.

Quite often when people want to fight, they're under the influence and suffering from some threat to their self-worth. If you want to handle them without fighting them, you let them have their dignity. Some guys, they've lost their wife, their job, their kids, and whatever. And they'll attack somebody over a minor remark. It might seem like a small thing to a normal person, but to that guy it's the only thing he has. He will fight to the death over it, so let him have his little moment of pride and he'll settle down.

The main thing to know about fighting is, take some training. Take some martial arts, especially if you're younger. It's good exercise, and there's a lot of stretching. And the beauty of martial arts is balance, so even older people should take martial arts because they'll find they walk better. They don't tend to trip and fall down as much. I took some martial arts for a couple of years. And although I never got a belt, I found that I had more confidence and better balance. Even if you're climbing up on a truck or a ladder and you do fall, you don't hurt yourself because you fall properly.

And training in the martial arts will teach you how to hit somebody.

Before I took martial arts, I was always off-target. I'd swing and miss the guy's jaw maybe two or three times before hitting him. If I did hit him, I'd throw him across the room, and yes, it looked spectacular. I'd hit the guy and he'd fly right across the room and then he'd jump up and come racing right back at me. But that's not what you want. When you hit a guy he's not supposed to move. The force is supposed to be disseminated throughout his body. When you throw him across the room, you don't hurt him. When you hit him and he drops, that's when you've hurt him.

You don't want the fight to go on and on, like it does in the movies. Guys smashing furniture, guys knocking each other across the room, that's all stupid. It doesn't work like that. You're not doing it for fun. In a long brawl, people start picking sides and jumping you from behind. You want it to be over in a few seconds.

So number one, you learn how to be on target with your fist or your foot. Number two, you learn to walk better, with better balance. And number three, you develop a distinctive sense of confidence, which other guys sense. And if they are really tough guys—guys with experience in fighting—they can sense that you know how to handle yourself. So they don't take liberties. The thing about fighting is, the better you get at it, the less likely you'll ever have to fight.

Once my friends realized that I was a good fighter, they would often try to stir things up just so they could watch the entertainment. But it was more entertaining for them than it was for me. I was once at this party and these drunk friends of mine were in the kitchen. They gave a guy a knife and told him to go out into the party and stab me. I can hardly believe that they did that, but there's no limit to the stupid things that people do when they're drinking. They knew that this guy was not going to be able to do me any harm with a knife. They just wanted to see the action. So this dumb idiot comes out of the kitchen and tries to stab me.

I did what you are supposed to do. I grabbed his wrist with my left hand and punched him with my right hand. The blade hit me in the hand and I hit him between the eyes. I got stabbed in the hand, but he went down like a sack of manure. If it weren't for my training I could've been in real trouble.

5

A DRIVEN MAN

"There's no limit to how far a man can go
in life if he doesn't ask permission."

By the time I was twenty-three or twenty-four years old I
was working like a madman, just trying to get ahead. The
partying and the wild times with my buddies were fading away.
I wanted to be a success. I was determined to be somebody.

I'd like to say it was my own decision to buckle down and
work hard, but it was how we were raised. When I was a kid in
school I was driven for high marks. My mum expected them
and my dad expected them. After a while it got so I expected
them, too. I didn't always get high marks, but I was never satisfied with poor marks.

In our family, you were expected to go hard and accom-
plish things. My dad made it as a paratrooper, and my aunts

and uncles risked their lives fighting for freedom in the Polish underground. My mum would talk to me about the people she admired, and they were always successful people. This one was a poet, this one was a writer. This one was a doctor and this one was a priest. She drilled into our heads that it was our job to go out and do something. So I always felt driven to succeed. So within my first year of arriving in Yellowknife I was basically working twenty-four hours a day.

I was driving a CAT in the daytime, bouncing at the Snowshoe in the evening, and working as a security guard at the Yellowknife Inn from midnight until eight in the morning. I also drove a taxi. At one point I was working four jobs seven days a week. I would sleep for half an hour behind the wheel if there were no taxi calls coming in, but basically I was just running on coffee and adrenaline and a couple of hours sleep here and there. My bouncing job technically went until one or two in the morning, but nobody at the inn got fussed up if I showed up a bit late for work, and even though I was only working about six hours they were still paying me for an eight-hour shift. They knew I was trying to dig my way out of debt, and in my experience everybody will get behind you if they can see that you are giving it your best shot.

So I was working, working, working, and the months were going by. In 1977, after a year in Yellowknife, I had cleared off all my debts and bought a mobile home. Louise had come up to join me at this point and our family was growing, with two small kids now—Shielo and Curtis. (We eventually would have eleven kids in all—Shielo, Curtis, Alex Jr., Nelson, Andrew, Dominic, Amelia, Julaine, Zeke, Ben, and Gianna.) One year later I sold that first mobile home and bought a brand-new one. Then I started buying older mobile homes and putting them on rental lots. I'd buy them for five thousand dollars, move them onto the lot, block them and level them, put porches on them, make the front of them look nice, maybe put some brick on them or some wood siding for decoration, clean up the interiors, make sure they were working good, and sell them.

Over the next three years I probably bought and sold sixteen of these mobile homes. My wife and kids moved up to Yellowknife and I made us a nice little home. I wasn't getting rich, but for the first time in my life I was holding both ends together, even if I couldn't quite get them tied.

The town was booming and I was making good money in the real estate business, so I probably should have stuck to it. But I get bored kind of easily, so I'm always trying something new, looking around for different ways to make money. I decided I would get into the livestock business. Why not? I was always going back and forth to Alberta and it seemed like a good idea to pick up some livestock while I was down there and bring it back to Yellowknife. People were always looking for fresh produce and fresh meat in these northern towns, so it seemed like a great idea.

So I brought chickens and ducks and roosters. I bought every big rooster I could get my hands on, and was getting fifteen bucks each for them. You could buy a chicken for a buck or two down south and sell them for ten bucks right away up here. Over time the city started jumping on us because these roosters crowed twenty-four hours a day, since it was daylight all the time. These poor things couldn't figure out when to start crowing and when to stop. The city wanted me to keep them in boxes and this and that. It got ridiculous, so we got rid of them and that was the end of that.

So I tried something else. My friend Danny the carpenter and a well-known lawyer named John Bailey and Harvey Selzer the electrician kept bugging me to bring up some pork on the hoof. "Why don't you bring us some pigs from the Peace River country when you go there?"

Okay, I'll go into the livestock business.

For pigs I needed a proper truck. There was this local guy by the name of Ed Gaukle. He was a contractor, wrote a children's book, and eventually committed suicide. Nice guy. I bought his truck—a '74 Ford one-ton. A nice-looking blue truck with an eight-foot deck on it. I put sides on it and went to Peace River and brought all these pigs back. Just little pigs, about twenty-five pounds. They're called wieners. I'd pay five or ten dollars for them down in Peace River and sell them for thirty-five in Yellowknife.

I didn't have to work at all to get rid of them. I'd be unloading these pigs behind Danny's carpentry shop and some guy would drive by with his pickup and say, "Hey, I'll take two of those."

So I sold him these pigs and fifteen minutes later he's back, saying, "Did my pigs come back?"

"What do you mean, 'Did your pigs come back?'?"

"They jumped out of the back of the pickup as I was going down the street."

"Oh, shit. I never even thought of it."

He'd just thrown them in the back of the pickup and drove away, and the pigs just bailed out.

I said to him, "Pigs aren't like dogs. They don't come back. These pigs have never been here before. They may show up in a month in Peace River."

I brought up bales of straw and pig feed to keep them, but as it turned out I didn't have to worry about food because most of my pig food came from restaurants. You wouldn't believe the perfectly good food that restaurants throw out every day.

I could have easily raised a hundred pigs just on restaurant garbage. Every city should have a pig farm and all those scraps should be going to the pigs. What a way to recycle!

I gave the cook at the hotel a bottle of whiskey, asking him to keep the food separated from the garbage, the cardboard and milk cartons and plastic wrappers and stuff because I just wanted the food for the pigs. So he did that for me. It worked out very well. One time there was a Black Forest cake at the top of the garbage can with a few slices out of it. I looked around to see if anybody was watching, took out my Leatherman, cut a chunk off, and had me a nice a slice of Black Forest cake. Another time, there was this huge arctic char. They'd had a banquet, ate half the char, and the rest of it they threw in the garbage. Nothing wrong with it. So I'm standing there by the garbage can eating a nice big chunk of this arctic char. I was kind of hoping that nobody was watching, but somebody fired a rock at me with a slingshot. It bounced around inside that shed where they keep the garbage. I guess these bums were watching me come and sift through the garbage every day, and they weren't too happy because I was competing with them for food. That was their main food supply. They were eating like kings, and then along comes this big Polack and starts eating their cake.

So I was selling these little pigs. Everybody wanted one. They are cute, too. I would tell people to feed them table scraps for a few months and then they would have themselves a real nice pig to butcher. But it's never as easy as it looks. Pigs pee a lot. The water goes right through them. And some people were complaining about the smell of the pigs, the way they root up the ground and turn everything into a swamp. And the little buggers are escape artists. Guys would take them home and in no time they would slip out of the yard and go running off. Before you knew it there were little pigs running all over town. So the bylaw officer who enforces the local laws was going nuts.

After a while people did not want to take them home alive. They wanted them butchered and ready to eat. So I had about fifteen of these pigs left and realized that I had to kill them myself. I felt really bad about that because these pigs and I got along real well. They were my little buddies. I would climb in the back of the truck where they lived, and they'd get all excited that I had come to see them, and they'd crowd all around me and I'd scratch them behind the ears.

But that's life. Pigs aren't pets, they're livestock. So even though I felt sorry for the little guys I went into the truck with a ball peen hammer and started cracking them on the head right between the eyes. The first one was pretty hard to do, but I got used to it and started butchering them right there in the driveway. The other ones didn't mind. They would just stand there and watch. I was boiling water inside the house because, of course, when you're butchering pigs you have to dip them in boiling water so the hair will come off. So I kept pouring boiling water into this barrel in the driveway and scraping the pigs. Then, of course, you have to open them up and remove all the innards and do a proper job of it. Let me tell you, that was quite a performance. I think the first one took me two hours. I used to butcher pigs when I was a kid on the farm, but I hadn't done it by myself for a long time, so it took quite a while to get the hang of it. But I think when I did the last pig I was down to about twenty minutes.

Now I've got all these butchered pigs and this barrel full of scrapings. It's too heavy to lift into the back of the truck and I can't figure out what to do with it. So I decide, to heck with it—it's the supper hour, nobody is around, so I'll just pour it into the road. My house is on the top of the hill, so I give the barrel a kick and this great cascade of hair and water and pig fat goes rolling down Bigelow Avenue. I'm thinking, *Good, that's all taken care of*, and I put the barrel away and go into the house to have some supper.

About halfway through supper I'm thinking, *What's that terrible racket?* I go and look out the door and here's a mob of ravens stretching all the way down the hill. That river of water and pig fat had run a couple of hundred feet down the hill. The ravens were lined up in a perfect row, fighting and feasting on those juicy little tidbits and making a heck of a racket. As I looked down the hill I saw my other neighbors standing in their doorways sticking their heads out looking at this lineup of a hundred or so ravens leading right up the hill to my driveway.

I guess they were thinking, *What the heck has Debogorski done this time?*

My backyard was basically like a zoo, and the city was getting mad at me. We had only one bylaw officer. Some people called her Billy the Terror. I called her Billy Bylaw. She was a big woman, as big as me, more than six feet tall, with big shoulders and Ukrainian blood in her. The first time I saw her she was jogging up the airport road on a hot summer day. She was coming toward me up that Jackfish Hill with the heat coming off the pavement, and I swear you could see the asphalt breaking under her feet. I figured, *Holy mackerel, that's one good-looking lady.*

Billy Bylaw was nobody to be messed with. If she ever practiced favoritism, you'd never know it, because she treated everybody equally badly. She showed up this one time and I had the pigs enclosed in three sheets of plywood against the wall of the trailer. We had a lamb in there, too, because we had butchered its brother and now it was running around the yard all the time going *bah bah bah* looking for the other lamb. So

I had put that lamb in with the pigs and it was happy to have the company. But it was a noisy little bugger and I hoped that it wouldn't start bleating while Billy was standing there.

She says, "I don't mind those chickens and ducks, but you better not have any pigs here."

"Oh, no, Billy, I have no pigs. Just a few birds."

And of course the pigs and the lamb are only forty feet away and I'm hoping that the sheep doesn't go *bah*, or that one of the pigs doesn't step on another, which always sets off a lot of squealing.

Shielo Debogorski

I'm Alex's daughter, the oldest one in the family. They say the firstborn kid has to break the trail for the other ones, and I believe it. My dad didn't exactly coddle us. I remember when we were little, if we were making a big fuss in the car, he would drop us by the side of the road and just drive away, leaving us in the middle of the wilderness. Then he would come back about ten minutes later. That usually did the trick.

When I got to be sixteen, we had this yard full of old cars and I thought that Dad should fix one up for me. He pointed out this old 1979 Ford Fairmont and handed me a shop manual and a box of tools. "There you go. Fix it up." He would never show you how to do anything. He would just expect you to figure it out by yourself. Around that same time he got hired to break up this old mobile home and haul it to the dump. It had been in a fire and it was a write-off. "Come on," he said. "You can help me." We drove over there with the truck and a backhoe and he told me to climb into the backhoe. He said, "This lever makes the bucket go up and down and this lever makes it go sideways. Just knock the trailer apart and load into the back of the dump truck."

I thought, *I'm sixteen years old! I have no idea what I'm doing!* As soon as he left I stepped on the gas and accidentally drove right into the dump truck and put a big dent in it. I knew that he would be mad at me, but I was even madder at him. And when he got back I started jumping up and down and yelling at him. He just stood there with a big grin on his face.

Then it was time for me to go away to college. He had this motorcycle and he arranged to get a photograph taken of himself in a muscle shirt, standing beside the bike, looking tough. Then he turned the photograph into a poster and had it laminated and ordered me to put it on the door of my room at college so that it would scare the boys away. He would drive all way down from Yellowknife without warning and show up at my door in the middle of the night. The first year, he must've done that about five times. Then he would take my friends to the bar and entertain them with stories.

When Norm and I announced our wedding, my dad put a big notice in the Yellowknife newspaper with a photograph of a grumpy old man in a rocking chair with a shotgun across his knees. My future husband was not amused. But it was just Dad's way of breaking him in. My dad likes reminding people that nobody gets a free ride. I remember all those summer days when we were kids, and our friends were out having fun, and Dad would make us go out to the topsoil pile to pick roots. He said he had to do it when he was a kid, and now we had to do it. Boy, it was hot and dirty. But he taught us how to work. And after that my other jobs seemed pretty easy.

Norm Fillion

I first met Shielo at the Gold Range Bar in Yellowknife. The bar might not be the best place to start a good relationship, but I really liked her. When we started dating, a lot of guys said to me, "That's Alex Debogorski's daughter. He's a great big tough guy. I've seen him fight, and you don't want to get on his bad side."

But I was serious about her. One thing led to another, and we had premarital sex, and she got pregnant. Now what? Alex and the whole family are Catholics, and I knew he wasn't going to be too happy about this news. I had a job up at the Distant Early Warning line in the Arctic, and I wanted to meet with Alex and have a talk before I went away for three months. Shielo thought that was a bad idea. I guess she knew her dad better than I did, and she was afraid of what he was going to do to me.

She won the argument, and I went up north. And when I got back she was starting to show her pregnancy and she had told her parents. I couldn't put off my man-to-man talk with Alex any longer, so I went up to the job site where he was working on a backhoe. Everybody had warned me that he was basically going to take me apart, but I figured I might as well take my medicine. I climbed up on the machine and asked him if we could talk. He turned off the engine and listened.

I told him I wanted to do the right thing, get married, and support my family. He nodded in agreement to all this, but he said one thing that stuck in my mind. It wasn't exactly a warning, but it made a strong impression. He said, "I don't want my daughter left alone with three kids, all used up, sitting in the Gold Range looking for another guy."

He has a knack for summing up all his concerns in one sentence. He loves his daughter and he'll back you up all the way as long as you do a good job as a husband. You can't ask for anything more from a father-in-law.

"What Kind of Dog Is That?"

The best pig we ever owned was a cross between a Vietnamese potbellied pig and a Russian wild boar. We got her in 2000. She grew to four hundred pounds and was covered with curly black hair. We called her Oink.

She was a big, hairy, impressive animal. She lived outside and roamed the neighborhood looking for things to eat. She would eat everything, including the tires off cars. Some people liked Oink and would feed her, so of course she got in the habit of approaching anyone she saw. If people didn't know her, she'd tend to scare the hell out of them. One time Oink approached a guy who was walking down the road, and the guy jumped into a flooded ditch. It was freezing cold and the guy stood in hip-deep water for about half an hour until someone came along and told him the pig was harmless. All the time Oink was standing there staring at him with these fierce little eyes and big razor-sharp tusks sticking out.

Another time a Mountie came to the house, and Oink cornered him. The cop retreated to the top of the front steps and stayed there until one of the kids came along and shooed the pig away.

Even dogs were afraid of Oink. You could see them cowering under their porches when she came trotting down the street. And this was the most mild-mannered animal. The kids taught her to climb stairs so she could come in the house. Great, I'd come home and there would be a pig the size of a compact car lying on the couch. My wife, Louise, didn't know what to do. I said to her, "She's just a pig, for Pete's sake. Show her who's boss."

The next time Oink started coming up the stairs Louise whacked her with a broom, and she fell all the way down the stairs. I don't think it hurt her, but she was impressed enough that she stayed off the stairs.

She was basically wild. Oink lived at our place, but she had free run of the neighborhood and we never penned her up. I don't believe in penning up animals. Let them run free and take their chances. So I was always getting in trouble with the city.

Billy Bylaw would come and see me. "Okay, I can't get you on the roosters, but you have to do something about that pig."

"What can I do? She's a wild animal. I basically don't even own her. She just comes and hangs out here."

"Don't bullshit me, Debogorski. I know she's your pig. Pen her up."

"You try penning her up. Have you seen her teeth? She could eat your patrol car."

I didn't want to push her too far. Bylaw was not someone you messed with. So I built a pen out of pallets lashed together with heavy-gauge steel wire. I put Oink in the pen and she just looked at me. I left, and she bit through the wire like it was dental floss and went off to panhandle the neighborhood. She never hurt anyone, but she cost me a fortune. There was a vet down the street with pet food supplies, and Oink would hide, watching for her chance. You'd just see this black beady eye peering around the corner of the building ready to eat up what she could find.

One time she ate up $254 worth of dog food in one shot. Another time she ripped open a dozen bags of kitty litter, hoping there was food in there. Obviously she couldn't read.

I wore a radio on my belt because one of my many sidelines was the topsoil business, and all day long the radio would be squawking with people complaining about Oink. "Your pig ate my groceries! That animal of yours is in the schoolyard again! There's a bear in my garden!"

One day this Native woman pulled into our yard and squinted at Oink through the window. There was no way she was getting out of the car. "What kind of dog is that?"

That gave us an idea. They have different competitions in the Yellowknife Spring Carnival, so we entered her in the "Ugly Dog" category. When the judges were finished deliberating they awarded her the prize for 1st Most Ugly Dog and 2nd Most Ugly Dog.

Oink finally died at the age of three. We suspect that someone poisoned her. I fired up the backhoe and buried her in the yard. The only place with enough soil was right under our bedroom window. Louise said, "Where did you bury Oink?"

"Never mind."

For quite a while afterward we'd be sleeping, and Louise would sit bolt upright in bed.

I'd say, "What's the matter?"

"I can hear her oinking."

"You're just imagining it."

"No, I swear I just heard her oinking out in the yard."

We were being haunted by the ghost of a pig.

My Growing Family

For some reason, working-class white families are having fewer and fewer kids. What's that all about?

People will say, "We can't afford to have more than two kids."

So at what point in history could people afford to have a lot of kids? Do you think the pioneers could afford large families? Do you think the farmers with one little tractor and a couple of horses could afford to have a large family? The fact is, people have never been able to afford large families. The previous generations recognized a simple truth—kids are not a liability, they are an asset. People have to turn their thinking upside down.

My aboriginal friend Richard Cadieux says we'd better watch out because the population of Indians is growing like crazy and we white people are having small families. And he's right. The aboriginal people know that kids are a joy. Money isn't important. People are important. And your family is your only true wealth in this world.

So by now I was in my late twenties and life was good. I was making some money. I had built a comfortable little home, and Louise and I were doing our best to repair the breeding imbalance of working-class white people by raising a whole mess of little Polacks—Shielo, Curtis, Alexander, Nelson, Andrew, Dominic, Amelia, Julaine, Ezekiel, Benjamin, and Gianna. We were working hard and playing hard. Yellowknife is a fun town. Nobody gets on your case. Everybody speaks their mind. There's a bartender in Yellowknife who keeps a special bottle tucked away for me under the counter. He's never told me what's in it—he claims it's a secret blend. But he gets it out and gives the air a good misting whenever I walk into his place. He calls it Polack Repellent.

There's no political correctness in this town. You can joke about anything. You could be any kind of oddball and everyone would leave you alone. We've got a sizable gay community in Yellowknife, for example. Everybody thinks Northerners are a bunch of rednecks and we're not going to tolerate a homosexual lifestyle, but it's not like that. The North is full of people who wind up here because they can't fit in anywhere else. I'm not in favor of the homosexual lifestyle, but I'm a big believer in personal liberty. You live your life, and I will live mine. I'm a conservative, but that doesn't mean I support hypocrites in conservative clothes. How can you say you believe in liberty and small government and then keep bugging the government to pass laws against people you don't agree with? I take the dirty old cow pie approach to the government. If they leave me alone, I just lay there not bothering anyone. But if they step on me I raise a big stink and they have a hard time cleaning me off.

One time I was at a wedding, and there was this gay guy there. Nice guy, worked in the mine. All the miners knew he was gay and they didn't give a damn. Anyway, I asked him to dance. We were waltzing around the floor, having a grand old time, but I guess he thought it was some ass-backwards way of making fun of him, because he gave up on me halfway through the song and went and found himself a woman to dance with!

Sports

Yellowknife also has a number of good sports teams. I gravitated to broomball. I like it because it's a violent game—all these big, tough guys running around clubbing each other with brooms. The referees were always carting guys off the ice. When I joined the team it wasn't doing very well. I thought, *We need to do a better job of intimidating the other teams.* So I decided to start growling. I would go into the corner with guys and growl like a werewolf.

The guys on the other team would say, "Why is that guy growling? Has he got a screw loose or something?"

It started freaking out the opponents. We went to this game in Hay River and my teammates started growling. It seemed to work, and we went on to become one of the best broomball teams in Canada.

In 1981 I also started competing in the spring carnival. There were all kinds of competitions—log sawing, muskrat skinning, arm wrestling, you name it. In one competition, the tea boiling, you had to start from scratch with nothing but a match and a kettle and a bunch of wood. Right off the start you had to make some kindling, start a fire, and get that teapot boiling. It sounds easy but let me tell you, when it's 30 below zero, getting a campfire started and boiling tea is a bit of a challenge.

They would also get you to carry heavy weights. They'd fill these backpacks with rocks and you were supposed to run around this obstacle course. All those skills I picked up as a boy came in handy, and it felt pretty good to be better than everybody else. Quite a few times I was crowned King Caribou—the champion of the Yellowknife Spring Carnival—and they sent me down to Edmonton to compete in the King of the Klondike.

That involved the same kind of stuff—lumberjack competitions, canoe racing, and so on, but with real serious competitors. It drew big crowds, and you could win four thousand dollars. Well, I was up against guys who literally practiced every day all year. Strong, tough guys with big shoulders and six-pack waists. They looked like they were on steroids or something. And here's big, clumsy Alex the Polack from Yellowknife. In one race, you had to throw a canoe on your head, run down a hill, and paddle it half a mile across a lake and back. I was competing against fifteen other canoeists who'd been practicing for months. I wasn't thinking that I was going to beat these guys—I was just thinking, *I don't want to come in last.*

When I came in third I felt like I'd won.

I liked the prize money, and I liked the feeling of showing these guys that I wasn't the class clown. But most of all, I liked entertaining the crowd. When you were a competitor they made a big fuss over you. They put you in a fancy hotel room and interviewed you. They put a camera on you and asked you questions. A lot of people got nervous, but I just figured, why not go for it? I would say a lot of things that were pretty outrageous.

The TV people would laugh, and afterward they would slap me on the back and say, "That was great. How do you spell that name again?"

I guess that's when I first started to think of myself as a character.

Andrew Debogorski

When I was a little boy my dad always told us not to complain about the little nicks and bruises you get while you work.

One time we were doing a cleanup job at this mine. The spill was contained by a line of straw bales and Dad was scooping them up with a front-end loader. He gave me a razor knife and told me to cut the bales so he could scoop them up. But about every third or fourth straw bale had a wasps' nest in it. As soon as I would cut open the bale, the wasps would come boiling out and attack me. I was getting stung pretty regularly, but Dad didn't seem to care. He thought it was hilarious.

He was way harder on himself than he was on us. Another time we were working in the shop, stripping copper with a disk grinder. He was getting me to help him, but he didn't like the way I was doing it. "Put on some thick gloves," he said. "You're going to cut yourself."

He gave me his gloves and then he kept working with his bare hands. A few minutes later I heard him say, "Ouch."

"What happened?"

"Nothing," he said. "I just cut myself."

I walked over to look at his cut and screamed in alarm. There was blood all over the place and his hand was cut right down to the bone. I grabbed his arm. "You have to go to the hospital!"

"It's nothing," he said. "I'll go later."

He kept working on the job. When he was finished, he went to the emergency ward and got his hand stitched up.

My Short Career as a Househusband

So this one time Louise went off to Edmonton on an errand and left the kids with my sister. I carried on with my normal life, working all day and fussing around with this and that, until one day my sister comes over with a car full of kids. I guess she's a little peeved that she's stuck with the babysitting just because she's a woman and I'm free as a bird just because I'm a man.

So I tell her, "Fine, leave the kids with me. I'm perfectly capable of taking care of the little varmints."

I'm thinking, *How hard can it be?* Compared to real work, babysitting is a breeze. So I plunge into the household chores.

I'm cooking, I'm cleaning. I'm sweeping the floors. In my opinion the house looks pretty darn good, maybe even better than it usually does. It's a school night, so I get them all tucked into bed on time, and in the morning I get them out of bed and make sure they're dressed properly, feed them their breakfast, make their lunches, find their boots, find their mitts, get their coats on, get them off to the bus on time, and then I'm left with the three-year-old and the five-year-old, who apparently are both too young to be in school.

So I tell them to go off and amuse themselves and stop bugging me, and I start cleaning the breakfast dishes. Man, these kids make an awful mess, but that's okay. I'm doing a heck of a good job washing the dishes and I'm just getting ready to dry them when the five-year-old comes into the kitchen and says, "Daddy, Daddy, there's smoke!!"

"What are you talking about?"

"Daddy, there's smoke!"

He points at the doorway into the bedroom, and sure enough, there's smoke pouring out of the door.

What the hell have they done now?

I rush into the bedroom and the bed is on fire. There's a disposable lighter lying on the floor and the bottom bunk is all in flames. So I run into the kitchen. Where's the fire extinguisher? I can't find the damn fire extinguisher. I grab a pot and start filling it with water. Do you know how slowly that sink pours water when your house is on fire?

Fill the pot, run into the bedroom, throw it on the fire. Doesn't do a damn bit of good. I make the kids stand by the front door while I keep throwing pots of water on the fire. But after a minute or two I can see that it's not going to be enough to put the fire out. If I was by myself, I'd open the window and start throwing the burning stuff outside, but I'm nervous with the kids there, so I just say to hell with it, and off we go outside.

I run down to the shop and call the fire department and they get there pretty quick, but by then the trailer is burning from end to end and it's too late to save it. Then I call Louise and tell her we've lost the house. "It's gone," I tell her. "There was no time to save a thing."

"How did it start?"

I tell her that the kids were playing with a lighter.

She thinks I'm joking. This is the part that kind of annoys me. I mean, how many times in our marriage have I joked with her about something so serious? I guess she can't believe that I can't keep an eye on the kids for more than twenty-four hours without one of them burning the house down.

My First Truck

I always wanted to own a big truck.

After my successes in the real estate business, I was ready to diversify. So I went down to an auction in Hay River, on the south side of Great Slave Lake, where the department of highways was getting rid of a lot of surplus equipment. I sat in on the auction and bought some good stuff—a dump truck, a track loader, a Bobcat, and a few other items. When the auction was over they wouldn't take my check, because they didn't know me, and told me I would have to go back to Yellowknife and get my check certified. That was a big hassle because by road the bank was over three hundred miles away. So I was kind of pissed off, feeling like I had come all this way, and now nobody trusted me to even pay for the stuff. You have to spend quite a bit of time in the North before they stop thinking of you as an outsider.

I went down to the coffee shop and there were some old-timers in the trucking business sitting there. I sat down, we started talking, and I told them my story. Merv Townsend said, "Where's your check?"

I took it out of my pocket and gave it to him.

Merv Townsend was a big player in the fuel-hauling business and everybody respected him. He scribbled his name on the back and gave it back to me. "Show them that."

That was quite a vote of confidence, because Merv Townsend didn't know me from a hole in the ground, but I guess he sized me up and figured I was worth trusting. I took the check back to the auctioneer and gave it to him. He turned it over and looked at the back and said, "Thank you very much, Mr. Debogorski, you can take your equipment now."

So off I went, with that old dump truck. It ran like a clock, even though it didn't have power steering. I hauled asphalt with it, and gravel and mine muck, and boy, I started building some upper-body strength handling that thing.

Eventually that old truck started burning oil really bad, so I loaded it up with an engine additive that seals up the engine pretty good but smells so bad that I would take one street when I was hauling a load out and take another street coming back just so that people wouldn't get mad at me. One time I was working through the supper hour, driving through this neighborhood, and this one fellow came out and said, "You know, that truck of yours smells so bad that I just tried to eat a hamburger and it tasted like shit."

Not too much later I had my first experience driving that heavily loaded truck onto a frozen lake. There were some guys who needed gravel out on Prelude Lake. I guess they wanted to build some driveways and I told them I would haul it out across the lake for them. I had never crossed unknown ice in a big truck and I was pretty nervous about it. If that truck broke through, I knew it was very unlikely that I'd be able to jump free in time.

I talked to some local boys about it. They said, "You should be fine." It's sort of a macho thing. Guys always say, "You'll be fine." People die every winter going through the ice, but everybody keeps slapping each other on the back and saying, "You'll be fine."

It was easy for them to talk because they'd only been driving across the lake in light pickup trucks. I didn't have much choice at this point because I'd agreed to do the job. I needed the money. So I loaded up the truck and eased it down onto the lake. I could hear the ice cracking under the wheels as I started out across that lake, trying not to think about all that water right underneath me. It was my first experience with ice road trucking. And I don't mind telling you, it scared the pants off me.

6

INTO THE
KINGDOM OF ICE

"It's man and iron against the elements
out here: either fix 'er or hold the light."

Driving a big truck across a frozen lake might seem like a
dumb idea, but nobody does it because they enjoy risk-
ing their lives. It's pretty much a necessity. If there was no such
thing as ice roads, there would be no such thing as economic
development in the Far North. And if there was no economic
development in the North, we would never get access to all
the oil and natural gas and minerals that are buried up here.

Let me give you a quick geography lesson. The Northwest
Territories are about twice as big as Texas but have only about
42,000 residents and about 550 miles of paved road. The terrain is all but impassable for much of the year, a vast wilderness
of lakes, forest, and spongy tundra devoid of trees.

John Denison

After the war was over I bought this old four-wheel-drive army truck in Yellowknife. That was when there was no highway yet. We met these people who were in the freight forwarding business and they used to hire CATs to haul stuff across Great Slave Lake.

We decided to try and do it by truck. It was faster than crawling along on an old CAT. We didn't have any windows in that old army truck. We were ten days on Great Slave Lake—went straight across to Outpost Island as quick as we could. All we had to cook with was a frying pan and some frozen eggs, and we used a blowtorch to cook the eggs.

In 1959 we put in a winter road to Fort Simpson, and in the winter of 1963 we built an ice road into Discovery Mine, 60 miles north of Yellowknife. It was mostly just me and two Natives that did it. We hauled up some houses all the way through the bush from Rayrock Mine to Discovery Mine. The houses were 24 feet wide and 40 feet long. In the years after, I built more ice roads, including a three-hundred-mile-long ice road up into Great Bear Lake.

I sometimes wonder now how the hell I did it. If I knew then what I know now there was no way I would do it. Everybody else told me I couldn't do it, but if you take no for an answer, how are you going to know you can or can't do it?

It's incredibly expensive to do any kind of construction up here, and even if governments and resource companies can afford to build roads, you could only go for a few miles in any direction without running into water. That's because the ground is always frozen and the water has nowhere to go. If you get up

in an airplane you can see that the terrain is pretty much splat-
tered with water—lakes and rivers as far as you can see—so it's
no wonder that the aboriginal people who lived here for thousands of years never bothered inventing the wheel. About the
only thing you could do with a wheel in these parts is sit on it
so you won't get your ass wet.

The Indians and Eskimos used canoes and kayaks for getting around in the summer, and they used snowshoes and dog
teams for getting around in the winter. By the way, before we
go any further, I have to say a word or two here about my
redneck terminology. I'm not trying to piss anybody off, but
I've done a lot of reading, a lot of research, and when I use
a word like *Eskimo*, it's not because I don't know any better.
A few years ago, somebody in Canada decided that the word
Eskimo was insulting. I don't know exactly where they got that
idea. Maybe someone at the CBC got upset because the word
Eskimo is supposed to mean "eaters of raw meat." Well, that's
exactly what they do eat, and it's a darn good diet. I wonder if
people in Toronto would be insulted if we called them "eaters
of raw sushi."

The point is, *Eskimo* is a perfectly good word that describes
all the aboriginal people who live in the high Arctic. They are
"Eskimoan" peoples. Words like "Inuit" refer to their language
groups. So if you are an Inuit you are an Eskimo. But if you
are an Eskimo you are not necessarily an Inuit. You might be
an Inupiaq if you live in Alaska, a Yupik if you live in Siberia,
or an Aleut if you live in the Aleutian Islands. But they're all
Eskimos, and they are proud to call themselves that. If any
of you politically correct types think that the word *Eskimo* is an
insult, I know a few tough Eskimo guys from Alaska who would
like to have a word or two with you.

Anyway, there's no shortage of know-it-alls in any period
of history, and when the Europeans first started showing up

in North America, they brought with them the same kind of smug assumptions about their own sophistication and superiority. The smart explorers learned from the natives and adapted their clothing, diet, and methods of transportation. The stubborn ones stuck to their own ways of doing things, and most of the time they paid for their ignorance with their lives.

That's what happened to the Sir John Franklin expedition, which took off from England in the spring of 1845 with 134 men. Franklin was looking for the Northwest Passage—a sea route through the treacherous icy waters of northern Canada. The Northwest Passage would shorten the distance between Britain and Asia, and any man who found it would be rich and famous for all time. Franklin's two ships were state-of-the-art for the time—they had heated floors, reinforced hulls, and were stocked with all the technology of modern British civilization. The officers had charts, telescopes, watches, compasses, uniforms, cutlasses, and all kinds of other crap that wouldn't do them a bit of good once they were a few weeks' sailing distance away from home. They imagined their ships to be floating versions of English society. The British officers didn't bother consulting with the Eskimo hunters they met when they arrived in the Arctic waters. They couldn't imagine that these dirty, illiterate people had anything to teach them about survival in the North. This was a big mistake.

The Englishmen spent several years blundering around in the ice-choked waters of the northern Arctic, and then the ships were crushed by ice and the sailors wandered off to find other white men who might help them. Of course, there were no white men for thousands of miles. At different times they ran into aboriginal hunting parties who could've saved them. The Eskimos have of course lived in the Arctic for thousands of years. They were perfectly comfortable there and still are.

They know how to stay warm and hunt the abundant wildlife and fish that live right under the ice.

The Englishmen walked for hundreds of miles, slowly starving to death, not realizing that food was right underfoot. Different groups of hunters offered the Englishmen seal meat and shelter, but the Englishmen wanted nothing to do with the "huskies," as they called them, and ended up dying in horrible conditions, finally eating one another in a desperate effort to stay alive—I guess it turned out that they weren't that fussy in their eating habits after all. I guess you could also say they didn't die of starvation, they died of stupidity.

So the key to surviving up here in the North has always been adaptability. The Indians and Eskimos knew that the easiest way to travel in this country is over water. So they adapted to that, and invented technologies that would allow them to travel over the water in the summertime by canoe and kayak, and in the wintertime by snowshoe and dog team. They never used horses or livestock in the North because there's nothing to feed them. They used dogs, and fed them with the cast-off meat scraps of the animals they hunted. About a hundred years ago, when gold prospectors flooded into Alaska and the Yukon, they learned from the natives and used a lot of their same methods for staying alive. During World War II, the surveyors of the Alaska Highway didn't have a clue where they were going. They used Indian guides to take them along traditional trails through the wilderness. These old Indian trails followed the land contours and valleys and showed the surveyors the easiest routes through some very rugged and difficult country, and the route became one of the most famous highway-building projects in history.

When prospectors and mining companies began opening up the North they were faced with a major problem—how could they move their heavy supplies into and out of country that had no roads? People down south might say, What's the matter with airplanes or helicopters?

Well, the problem is money. It takes a lot of money to build a landing strip for an airplane. How are you going to get the bulldozers up into some of these remote camps? And the drilling camps they use for mineral exploration tend to move around a lot. You can't build a new airstrip every time you build a new drilling camp. You could move stuff in and out by floatplane, but floatplanes are small and can't carry very much. Helicopters are even more expensive, at least a thousand dollars an hour. Mining supplies are heavy and bulky, and it's so expensive to transport anything by airplane that economic development of the North would not have been possible if someone hadn't come up with a solution.

Tom Berry, a snowplow operator in John Denison's original road crew

John Denison proved that freighting with standard trucks right up into the Arctic is feasible. Take a load of lumber straight from Vancouver to Port Radium! Why not? This kind of operation is making this country! When he started hauling freight in trucks successfully this far north, even into the Barren Lands, he was the only man in the Territories doing it. Everybody said he was nuts. Everybody.

The man who really pioneered the concept of the winter ice road was John Denison. He started off working as a police officer in the Mounties, but he got tired of following orders and went off to work for himself as a remote-road builder. It's a good thing he did, or there might never be a show like *Ice Road Truckers*.

From the 1950s to the 1970s John Denison learned just about everything there is to know about building roads across frozen lakes. He learned, for example, that snow is your worst enemy when you are trying to build a good ice road. Snow puts an insulating layer on top of the ice, and it's impossible for the cold to get right down into the road. So he plowed the snow off the ice roads and even pumped water onto the road to make the ice thicker. He learned also that you have to make an ice road really wide or else every time the wind picks up the snow will drift into the roadway and it has to be plowed out again. If it's wide, the snow drifts right across. It's the same principle as a flat roof. You'd think the snow would build up, but the wind cleans it off.

He also pioneered an interesting way to build a ramp from the lake surface up onto the shore. Sometimes there's a drop of three or four feet from the land onto the lake surface. Instead of messing with planks and logs, he would build a ramp out of snow and soak it with water, adding one layer after another until it was hard as rock. He deliberately built his roads on the ice wherever he could, because it's flat and easy going on the lakes, and built short passages through the bush when he had to go from one lake to the other. He called these short overland routes "portages." It's a French word that comes from the old fur traders who used to travel these routes and haul the canoes on their backs across the portage trails from one lake to another. Even with all the things that John Denison learned, it was very dangerous work, and his vehicles sometimes crashed through the ice, sometimes taking one of his drivers down with it.

In the 1960s, a writer from the *New Yorker* heard about John Denison and his ice roads in the Canadian Arctic. Her name was Edith Iglauer. She was a city girl but a good journalist, and she traveled up into northern Canada to spend time with

John Denison while he built a three-hundred-mile-long road above the Arctic Circle. You had to hand it to her—it was pretty tough cohabiting with all these rough men in winter bush camps where there really wasn't even a way to wash yourself, let alone a place to dress or use a proper toilet. And by all accounts John Denison was a crusty and hard-driving man. Still, he and Edith ended up respecting each other, and she produced *Denison's Ice Road*—a book that soon became a classic, and did a great job of explaining how Denison's ice roads were going to make it possible to explore the North and extract its gas, oil, diamonds, and gold.

Northern resource development starts with prospecting. Having been a gold prospector myself when I was a young man, I can tell you that it is a tough and risky proposition. We would never get anywhere without the prospector, but most of the time the prospector gets nothing for his money. Still, it's the dream of hitting it big that keeps him slugging it out, living in the bush, eating bad food, fighting bugs, and hoping that Lady Luck is going to smile on him one day.

Charles Fipke and Stu Blesson were prospectors of this kind. Fipke was obsessed with finding diamonds in the North even though everyone said he was crazy. He teamed up with this geology professor from South Africa, and they started tracking little particles of this type of rock called kimberlite that had been scattered across hundreds of miles of open terrain by glaciers thousands of years ago. It was like a Sherlock Holmes mystery. What they needed to do was follow the pieces of evidence, trying to track their way back to the source. Diamonds hide in kimberlite, and they followed this faint trail for 350 miles from the Mackenzie Valley to Lac de Gras. Finally he discovered diamonds around Lac de Gras, northeast of Yellowknife, and ended up making a fortune and owning a share of the Ekati Diamond Mine.

Fipke and Blusson's discovery launched the biggest prospecting stampede in North American history. My friend Gord Van Tighem, the mayor of Yellowknife, was a banker at the time and he says it was just pandemonium. The sky was full of helicopters and the lumberyards were running out of wood because prospectors were out there pounding stakes into every piece of exposed ground in the Northwest Territories. It made the Yukon Gold Rush look like a yard party.

Nowadays Canada is the third most important producer of diamonds in the world and produces well over a billion dollars' worth of diamonds every year. These mines require an enormous amount of material coming in and out every year, and that's how I got involved. A couple of different companies partnered up to build temporary winter ice roads to these mining camps, and they needed good truck drivers who could handle big rigs loaded with heavy and awkward equipment and haul these loads reliably through some pretty tough terrain and terrible weather conditions.

I've been involved in the whole diamond rush one way or another, from its beginning about twenty years ago. I helped Knut Rasmussen take the first bulk sample for Winspear, which became Snap Lake when DeBeers took it over. I trucked his equipment out to MacKay Lake on the ice and unloaded it on a snowbank. He had to push and drag it across country because there was no road to Snap Lake. Then I flew in and ran one of his Cats.

Having lived here in the North over thirty years and the North being what it is—underpopulated with fantastic potential—when big new developments occur, everyone has the option of being involved.

There aren't too many guys out there on the ice roads with as much time on their hour meter than me. Ice road trucking is good money—more than five hundred bucks a trip—and it's a short season, so there is no time for rest. When you have a family as large as mine, you are under constant pressure to keep the cash rolling in. My wife plans to work me to death, but I'm big and strong, so that's going to be a long, slow death for this Polack.

They start building the ice roads in early November. About a hundred and forty guys from a construction company called Nuna Logistics work through minus temperatures that get down to seventy below and nights that are twenty hours long. In early December, helicopters fly the route and crews stop to measure the ice depth. Once it's about twelve inches thick, these special tracked vehicles called Haglands drive out onto the portages to compress the snow and help the ground to freeze.

When the ice is sixteen inches thick, Sno-Cats go onto the lakes to clear away the snow so the cold temperatures can get right down into the ice. The road is flooded to help increase the depth. This is the most dangerous time on the ice road. It seems like every couple of years we have a fatality. A plate of ice will fracture and the vehicle will tip into the open water. The ice closes back over the hole and you're sealed underneath. The shore is also a bad place because of the sun and the thin ice, but at least the water is shallow there. When the ice is twenty-eight inches thick, the first trucks can go out, lightly loaded. Usually just a wheel or an axle will break through, and you'll jump out of the truck and wait inside the cab of another truck for the winch truck. You don't even want to fall through shallow ice, up to your knees or waist, because the shock of the cold water can stop your heart.

The ice gains thickness at about an inch every couple of days. Once there's a minimum of thirty-five inches of ice, the road is ready for full five- and six-axle loads. The biggest ice road in the world is the Tibbitt to Contwoyto Winter Road, a frozen highway that runs out of Yellowknife and goes 370 miles into the northern wilderness. It's as wide as an eight-lane highway and is the longest heavy-truck ice road in the world. But they still have to wait until late February, when the ice thickens to more than forty inches. By then it is strong enough to support the eight-axle "Super B" articulated trucks we drive back and forth to the mines.

The ice roads only last for about sixty days, so you have to go hard to make sure that the mines have all the freight and equipment they need to operate for the other ten months of the year. During the ice road trucking season, I concentrate on the ice road twenty-four hours a day. Every day revolves around getting eight hours sleep, getting the next load and delivering it, missing weather and accident tie-ups, and getting back to do it again. I have to be very efficient and disciplined to haul the maximum number of loads in this short time frame. Taking Valentine's Day or any other day off is not an option. In the old days before "risk aversion," thirty-six hours of continuous driving was not unusual for some of us. It sounds easy, but going every day for two months takes a lot of determination. Lots of the guys can't do it without taking days off.

It wasn't very long after Fipke and Blusson struck it rich that prospectors and entrepreneurs of every sort started flooding into Yellowknife, hoping to make their own fortune. Pretty soon you'd be running into people from all over the world—Tanzania, Mauritius, Armenia, India. Many of them came to work in the diamond industry, either cutting and polishing diamonds or working in the mines. Other people got jobs in construction or heavy equipment. The ones who were capable of hard work have succeeded and done well. The ones who are looking for a quick buck don't usually last more than a few months. Anyone with half a decent work ethic can come up here and make seventy or eighty grand a year as long as they don't mind hard work. But you have to be a digger. They're building a bridge over the Mackenzie River right now, and if you want to get an idea of the sort of work that people have to do up here, go down to that bridge and take a look. When it's pitch dark at nine o'clock in the morning, 35 below zero, you'll see guys who have been working outside for two hours already. You have to be a special breed of cat to make it in the North.

So now you've got these three big diamond mines, hundreds of miles north of Yellowknife, and if you climbed into the cab of my Mack truck one cold, black February morning I'd take you for a little ride and show you what ice road trucking is all about. The first thing you would probably notice is, we don't just drive across these lakes when it's necessary. We drive on them whenever we get a chance. The highway engineers who survey and design these ice roads deliberately build them on the lakes wherever it's possible. That's because they know what the Indians always knew—it's smooth going on the ice. The first couple of hours, driving north out of Yellowknife, we spend a lot of time on the land. And it can be rough going. You can go faster but you're going up and down hills and around corners, and the road is narrower so you really have to stay on your toes and make sure you don't run into some other guy who's taking more than his share of the road coming around a sharp corner.

Once we drive onto the ice, it's a different game.

Driving a heavily loaded truck down a hill and onto a frozen lake is easier than driving it down a mountain. But both are dangerous in their own way. The ice on top of a lake is flexible. It sags when it takes the weight of the truck, like a big trampoline. You're not going to notice it sitting up in the cab, but it definitely sinks a few inches as the truck drives onto it.

As we go across the lake, the truck will depress the ice and push a wave of water ahead of us. We need to go a certain speed, not too slow, not too fast. The road engineers will measure the thickness of the ice with sonar equipment and recommend an ideal speed. Trucks have to be a minimum of a third of a mile apart on the ice. They don't want us to stop, either, because the truck's stationary weight can damage the ice, and they don't want us going too fast because we're pushing that wave ahead of us. If we are going too fast all that water will hit the shore and cause a "blowout." That's when the ice erupts from underneath. Generally when a truck breaks the ice due to speeding, the tractor gets over but the trailer drops in. Often the offending truck goes over the wrecked ice, and the truck that is following goes into the hole. If the truck drops through fractured ice, we'll have to bail out as quickly as we can, because it will open up for the truck and then close up afterward. The ice closes over like a slab, but more often than not like a bunch of broken chunks. Should the driver get out of the cab after the truck lands at the bottom of the lake, the broken pieces of ice on the surface can be too much to push apart to reach the air.

Our biggest enemy here is actually the boredom. The long road is wide and straight, and some of the lakes are so wide they practically put you into a trance—especially at night, when one's gaze is trapped by the headlights. On top of that, you can only go about twenty miles an hour. We've got one lake called "Two-Movie Lake" because it takes two DVDs to cross it. But when you've been up and down this road as many times as I have, you never really relax. I'm always watching, waiting for something bad to happen. If the truck goes through the ice, you've got a couple of seconds to jump clear. We lost one twenty-three-year-old kid who was plowing an ice road, and his truck broke through and he drowned.

We also had a guy die when his plow broke through the ice on the Tibbitt to Contwoyto Winter Road. The other guys from Nuna pulled him out, but the water was so cold he died of a heart attack.

These guys would not have died if the ice had been thicker. It wasn't cold weather that killed them. It was warm weather. We've had some real warm winters over the last ten years. I think 2005 was the warmest winter in a hundred and fifty years. They closed the ice road early, about mid-March, because the ice started giving out. We have some lakes that are worse than others. So the engineers do their best to keep the road safe. They build the road so it comes ashore at an angle, so the wave going ahead of the truck will deflect off the shore and be less likely to cause a blowout. Every day, a crew drives along the road dragging an electronic unit that sends four-hundred-megahertz radio waves down into the lake. The signal bounces off the surface of the water, under the ice, and measures the thickness of the road. Nuna has crew workers drilling with power augers to check the ice visually. They've also got engineers who are trying to put together maps of the world under the ice road—the reefs, the sandbars, and the hidden currents that can change the strength of the road. The thing is, they know how ice acts in the lab. But here in nature, it's always changing. It flows and grows and shrinks and bulges by the day, affected by all kinds of forces the scientists don't really understand. Like all things in nature, it's a living thing.

Jim Chapman, owner of Byers Transport, Yellowknife

Our early drivers were daring fellows. Some of the drivers would drive on ice with the door open and stand on the running board and steer with one hand while the ice was bending underneath them. Very, very fortunate we never lost any men. We did lose, I guess, three complete units that went down at the bottom of Hottah Lake. We were never able to recover them. The bottom of those lakes is silty muck, about two feet deep. As soon as you touch anything it just riles up the muck and you can't see a thing.

The ice conditions at the time we lost those units were not bad. The ice was four feet thick, but it was so cracking cold! The ice was just as brittle as can be. Without warning a crack would open up in the ice and just run. The colder the temperature, the brittler the ice gets. I have stood on the edge of a lake and watched a crack and listened to it. They come in the distance just like thunder and you can hear it go ripping across the lake. Pretty soon you see a crack two to four feet wide.

And then when the weather turns warm and the ice starts to swell, the crack closes right up again. When it continues to get warm, the ice begins to pile. This is what you call an ice ridge. You are then either building bridges to take you across the cracks or chopping down huge mounds of ice to get through. Some of the ice ridges can be twenty-five feet high. The power of lake ice is just as powerful as tides in the ocean.

How dangerous is ice road trucking?

Well, we don't fall through the ice very often, like you might think. We've become pretty darn good at our jobs. The highway engineers know exactly what thickness of ice will support how much weight, and they know the best routes across each lake to avoid bad spots. They have sonar monitoring devices to keep tabs on the thickness of the ice on each section of the road. They operate the ice road for only about sixty days every year, so we're not taking chances and running heavy rigs too early or too late in the season.

But it's still dangerous. You're driving on ice. You see jack-knifed rigs, collisions with other trucks, smashups with ice ridges, avalanches, and rollovers on mountain roads. Hell, just the frostbite can cost you some ears or toes. So how dangerous is it? Just look at the fact that some rookies quit after a few days. That should answer the question.

There are some stretches of road that never freeze properly. So the road crews come up with some pretty interesting solutions, like putting down a network of steel and wooden beams called a "rig mat." Once that sucker is frozen into the ice they'll flood it with water to bridge the weak spot.

So we like cold weather up here. Usually when it's real cold—forty below—the sky is clear, and when the sun finally comes up it's actually kind of cheerful. We'll get these sunny mornings with blue skies, white snow, and well-defined shadows on the road so you can see holes and rough spots from a long way off. We'll get beautiful orange sunsets in the evening, and clear nights with incredible stars and northern lights. Then one day we'll see this cloudy band in the western sky. Looks like a long, gray scarf stretched across the horizon. That means the weather is going to get interesting, and not interesting in a good way.

On the ice road, falling snow and strong winds can cause a condition we call whiteout. The weather can change in minutes. The wind is coming across the road and we won't be able to see more than a few yards ahead. It's like being suspended in nothingness, like being caught inside a snow globe. We can put on yellow sunglasses to create some contrast, and drive slowly so that we're not coming up on any surprises in the road, but no matter what we do, a whiteout is a dangerous thing to drive in.

And it's dangerous no matter how good a driver you are. Rookie drivers come up here and say, "Well, this isn't so bad. The sky is nice and clear. The road is a hundred and fifty feet wide. There's no traffic to speak of. What's the fuss?"

They forget they're on a frozen lake and that the road is basically an ice rink. Doesn't affect them when they're rolling along in good weather. But then it starts to snow. The wind picks up, the visibility closes down, and now they're scared. Holy smokes, I can't see! A hole appears ahead or a curve comes up, they touch the brakes, and suddenly the truck turns into a fifty-ton curling rock. The trailer is coming up alongside them and they end up all knotted up, piling into a snowbank. A jackknife on top of Charlie's Hill caused the roof to pop off the unibody cab, and the new truck was written off. Ice road trucking is not as easy as it looks.

It's not just the rookies who get overconfident. I heard this one old-timer boast, "I've been in lots of whiteouts, but I've never lost control and put her in the ditch. Been driving thirty years, never hit a snowbank."

Wouldn't you know it, right after he made that announcement he put his truck into a snowbank, and I had to pull him out, and then he put her in the snowbank again, twice in the same day. I don't like tempting fate. Too many times, I've had the trailer skidding on ice, coming up alongside me. I've been in the snowbank a few times. A couple of those times there was no one to help me. It took a lot of shoveling and ingenuity to get out. I have pulled a lot of guys and even a girl out of the snowbank.

Some of these lakes are sixty miles long, and it takes three hours to drive across them. Guys tend to forget that they're even on a lake. It's like driving across the Great Plains—this big wide highway going as crooked as a dog's hind leg toward the horizon. That's when truckers attempt to make up a little bit of time by pushing their speed. Speeding is a real no-no on the ice road. Excessive speed is dangerous because you might jackknife on a slippery section or catch up with that wave that's running ahead of you just under the ice. If you catch up with it, you're going to break through. Speed is especially dangerous when you approach land. The wave hits the shore and comes back at you. If you're going too fast, you'll meet that wave head-on. You're thinking, *Now I'm safe, I can step on it*, but that's when you're most likely to break through. So you have to go nice and slow. It makes for a long trip. On some of these big lakes, you almost feel like getting out and jogging alongside the truck. It feels like you're moving that slow.

Up here in the North, the days are short in the wintertime. She's starting to get dusky by three in the afternoon, and you'll find that most of your driving on the ice road actually takes place in the darkness. If loneliness bothers you, you start to feel like you're the only person left out there. It's just you, the soft roar of the diesel, and the headlights probing through the darkness. On a cold winter night the ice never stops talking. You'll be amazed at the sounds you get from a frozen lake. Sometimes it rumbles like the stomach of the world's biggest cow. Then it squeals and chirps and moans. When the ice is happy it cracks when you drive a big truck across it. If the lake is cracking the old-timers say it's "making ice." Every time it cracks, it's a little stronger. Maybe the water is seeping into the cracks and freezing again. Whatever the reason, ice is stronger and thicker when you drive big trucks on it. So when I'm driving in a bad spot I'll sometimes leave the window open and listen for the cracking. It's not just so I can enjoy the sound of the ice, either—it's also so I can bail out the window if necessary.

After all these years I'm still not totally comfortable driving a heavy truck on the ice. And even though those cracking sounds are supposed to be good, it's still eerie listening to them, especially when it's your first run of the year and it's been some time since you heard the ice talking back.

With the window open you can really hear it. Loud cracks like artillery. The first time the rookies hear it, they think it's pretty terrifying. I've heard it a million times, but it still makes my stomach flinch. I know all that noise is good. It means the lake is making ice. But sometimes you hear that crack go off like thunder underneath the truck, and you can't help thinking, *Oh, boy, this is it.*

We learned a lot from old-time guys like John Denison. They put a lot of trucks through the ice before they learned about the dangers.

That Long and Lonesome Ice Road

Brief moments of terror separated by long hours of boredom. That's ice road trucking.

When you sit in one position for hour after hour you start to feel pieces of your body that you never knew were there. You get this one little muscle on your ass that starts to ache, then your ankle gets stiff, then you start wishing that you could just get out of the truck and stretch your legs and walk for a few minutes. But you can't. You're on a timetable and you've got to deliver a load. Everything is measured by the estimated time of delivery, and there's no time for strolling around.

For me, my right leg gets sore because I'm only going 15 miles an hour and the truck's cruise controls won't set that low. You have to be going 20 to 25 for cruise control to work. So you're riding that gas pedal all the time, making little adjustments, driving your leg crazy.

You don't have much choice because cruise control can be a bigger problem than it's worth. On these 35-mile-an-hour fast lanes, guys will start setting their cruise control at 35 and forget that they're on ice. Well, guess what? The truck starts going sideways. The truck doesn't know it's on ice, and cruise control tells its wheels to keep going 35 while the truck is going into a 360-degree spin into the snowbank. The next thing you know you have fifty tons of freight coming in the window.

I've been driving for a long time, but that doesn't mean I know all the tricks. One of the things I like about this job is that you're always learning. Every day you learn something. My old buddy Roman Welna there, he's made himself his own cruise control device. He's got a stick with a little notch in it that fits onto the gas pedal and makes the truck go just the right speed in that gear.

Roman likes to lead so he doesn't have to worry about running into the back of anybody. He just sets his stick in there and down the road he goes. If he gets into a skid the stick comes off in a second. It's never been a problem for him yet. The winter road people, they've got it all figured out how long it should take you to go between this portage and that portage, from Tibbett Lake to the Meadows and Dome Lake, and from Dome Lake to Lockhart and so on. They've got the times sorted out precisely. I've followed Roman and we've often come in right to the minute. I like driving behind him because it's like following a big wristwatch.

I have spent more than a few hours on the radio telling stories to these rookie drivers from the South. I tell them about the strange and exotic animals they are going to meet in the North. We have these special types of Arctic flies, for example. Insects can't survive out here at 40 below unless they grow a coat of hair, so our flies grow a nice thick coat of white fur. If the wind's blowing really hard the flies come drifting down from the North Pole. I tell the other truckers to watch really closely and they'll see these fur flies drifting along the ground.

I get a good chuckle out of imagining some of these guys stopping their trucks and running around in the snow trying to catch one of these furry little flies to take home as a souvenir to show their wives.

Then we've got our rare "fur fish."

Our local aboriginal guys know all about fur fish. When they are drilling holes in the ice to pump water up onto the ice road, every once in a while a furry-nosed little trout will stick its head up through the hole to see what's going on.

I can hear the truckers yelling at me, "Come on, Debogorski, you think we're going to believe that?"

"Use your common sense, man! You think it's easy for a fish to survive in these waters?

I also tell them about the new business that I'm starting up. It's a health food product—chocolate-covered caribou turds. I'm getting the stuff tested to see what it has for vitamin C and antioxidants and all the other good vitamins. It's perfect for putting on your porridge in the morning. I've got five tons of it stored in my machine shop. The government health department is getting involved and I've got a big venture capitalist behind the idea and pretty soon I'm putting my caribou turds on the market.

Now they are roaring in disbelief. "That's a lot of crap, Debogorski!"

"Yes, sir, it darn near fills my whole shop."

Then of course you've got your scary stories. It's spooky being out there in the middle of the night. The North is a powerful and spiritual place. Sometimes when you're driving on the ice road late at night, all by yourself, those northern lights start dancing overhead and you'd swear they're alive. Some people think the lights are the spirits of people who have died in the last little while, swirling around up there in the sky. I'm not saying I believe in spirits and ghosts, but if you live in the North you learn that there's a lot more to life than science can explain.

I tease some of the rookie drivers about some of the weird and frightening things they might encounter out on the ice road—snow snakes, Sasquatches, ice worms—and they kind of laugh because they think I'm kidding. But I can tell they're a little bit spooked, and who wouldn't be? You take any city person and put them out there in the Arctic night all by themselves and they'll soon be seeing funny things, too.

You've got the snow blowing across the road, two hundred feet of black water under your wheels, all ready to swallow you up in a heartbeat if the ice fails, and it's no wonder some guys get creeped out.

I try to reassure the other truckers by telling them what they can do to protect themselves against flying saucers and aliens. The guys who travel with me have heard these stories many times, but that doesn't make them immune. I'm telling you, put anybody out on MacKay Lake in the middle of the night and they're gonna start getting nervous. That particular lake is sixty miles long, so it's a three-hour drive at twenty miles an hour, and it's so dark and lonely out there, without a tree or rock or single sign of human life, that you start to feel like you're cruising along on a foreign planet. I enjoy driving across MacKay Lake in the middle of the night because it gives me a chance to pass on my safety tips to the younger truckers.

I tell them how the flying saucers come overhead and they go down and they take the drivers out of the trucks, take them up to the flying saucer and probe them.

That always gets a response from some rookie. "What the hell do you mean, 'probe them'?"

"Well, people who have survived it say that the aliens have these computerized instruments that they stick in various unmentionable parts of your body. They stick them in there, and suck out everything you know."

"That's crazy!"

"I'm just telling you what the experts say."

"How come we never see an abandoned truck, then?"

"They put an alien in behind the wheel so he can drive the truck across MacKay Lake. You ever see a truck acting kind of funny? Swerving around and skidding for no reason? That's a good sign that there's an alien driving it. The aliens have skinny little arms and they're not very experienced at driving fifty-ton trucks, especially on ice. Sometimes they'll lose control and end up in a snowbank."

I can tell by the silence at the other end of the radio that I've got everybody listening now.

"When that happens they pull the alien out of the truck and drop the driver back in. That's why it's such a shock when you find yourself in a snowbank. You know that feeling? You're just driving along, everything is fine, and suddenly you're in a snowbank! How did I get in a snowbank? Well, they were poking and prodding you up in the flying saucer, and then they had to transport you back to the truck when this incompetent buddy of theirs drove into the snowbank."

Finally they can't take it. "Oh, Debogorski, you're so full of shit. Where do you get these stupid stories? What's the matter with you?"

Now I'm real serious and I say, "Well, how many times have you driven across MacKay Lake and got to the north end, portage forty-nine, and think, *Holy mackerel, I don't even remember the trip! Was I asleep the whole time? It's like a blank!?*"

It's quiet on the radio. I say, "Well, the reason you don't remember the trip is because you've been up in a flying saucer getting prodded while an alien's been driving the truck."

I usually don't get too much comeback because now they're thinking, *"Damn, he's right."* I tell that story every year, and somebody always believes it.

I am like the older boy in the bunkhouse, trying to scare the younger ones with ghost stories. But sometimes the shoe is on the other foot. A strange thing happened one night when I was crossing Gordon Lake. It was the middle of the night, midnight or so, and I was heading home. After many days away I was looking forward to a bath, a hot meal, a visit with my wife, and a few hours of sleep before I headed north with another load. But then at the north end of Gordon, this voice comes over the radio. "I am watching you."

What?

In those days we had CB radios. All the drivers were running with CBs, so I thought the voice on the radio was this other truck driver named Dwayne I was traveling with in a two-truck convoy. But it didn't sound like him.

The voice comes on again. "I am watching you."

I said, "Dwayne, is that you?"

Dwayne came back, and said he didn't know what I was talking about. It wasn't his voice anyway. His transmission was all broken up with static. This transmission was nice and clear, from somebody real close by.

"I am watching you."

There was no one in sight, just stars and darkness. It was as spooky as hell. Somebody was watching me. That was it.

Are You Talking to Me?

I wish I had a nickel for every time I heard someone say something insulting about truck drivers. The stereotype is that your average trucker is some dumb guy with a grade-nine education who can't do anything else. Well, there's prejudice of all kinds out there, and that's just another version. People who talk like that are revealing more about their own ignorance than about the supposed ignorance of your average long-haul truck driver.

The fact is, driving a truck is a difficult, complicated, and demanding job. You're in charge of equipment that might be worth two hundred thousand dollars, hauling a load that might be worth well over a million dollars. You have to keep a whole lot of paperwork organized and up to date, and you have to know how to deal with the police, Customs, and truck inspectors. You're responsible for people's lives. You make one mistake, you could kill a lot of people. And in my opinion, most truckers are excellent and safety-conscious drivers. Whenever someone does something stupid on the highway, it's invariably a four-wheeler. If there's an accident involving a truck, it's almost always the four-wheeler's fault. Don't take my word for it. Check out the reports. Then ask yourself, When is the last time you saw a trucker do something as stupid as the things that car drivers do every day?

The bottom line is that it takes a lot of skill to drive a truck properly. You ever watch a guy back a semitrailer through a crowded parking lot and tuck it into a loading dock just a few inches wider than his wheels? I'd like to see the average person try it sometime. It would change their mind about who they're considering a low-skilled worker.

Adele Boucher, co-owner of Boucher Trucking, Peace River

There was that movie *Smokey and the Bandit* with Burt Reynolds. That gave trucking this cool look. It moved from cowboys to urban cowboys. Truckers became sexy after Burt Reynolds.

Bush and highway drivers are two different breeds. The highway drivers come in from the outside and they think they're going to show us bush apes a lot of things. But when one of those highway fellas has something happen to his truck, even though he knows how to repair it, he's not used to doing that, so he just sits and waits for someone to come along and fix it. Their first trip up here, these highway drivers don't even like to cross the Mackenzie River. The ice scares the hell out of them, and it's like prodding a cow onto an airplane to get them to go out on the ice.

You'd be surprised in this country how many trucking companies have farmers as employees. Everybody who works for us in the winter season is a farmer in the summer season. You get this upbringing on the farm, learning a little bit about machinery and the value of time. You do what has to be done when the sun shines. And you just apply that to the job. They are the most loyal people in most trucking companies. They know the value of a big piece of equipment.

Lots of people go through university, get a job at a bank or a big insurance company, and decide they want to drive a truck. It's good money, and you've got the freedom of the open road. You're not stuck in an office. You're seeing the world, and you can be your own boss most of the time. When I listen to the radio at night I sometimes feel like I'm attending school. You're always hearing things you never knew before. Mind you, it's not always the kind of stuff you'd want your kids listening to!

I remember this one time I was heading south and passed these two trucks going north. They were tankers, and the older guy in one truck was explaining certain things about sex to the younger guy in the other truck. This older guy knew everything, and I mean everything, about the human body, the reproductive system, and sexual activity. He was explaining the many, many ways a man can take a woman to whole new heights of sexual excitement, and I'm telling you, most of this was stuff you couldn't make up in your wildest dreams. I don't know if he was some kind of sex therapist or something, but I think every driver within a hundred miles was jotting down notes! You could have heard a pin drop on the radio that night! It was so interesting that when their radio signal started to fade I felt like turning around and following them just so I could hear the end of the conversation.

Another time, I was listening to these two truckers, and they were talking about what they were going to do with their money when they finished the ice road season. One guy said, "I think I'm going to rent a warehouse and grow marijuana."

The other guy said, "It's not as easy as you think. You have to really know what you're doing."

"It can't be that hard. Every bozo in Vancouver is growing weed."

"Yeah, but they're getting caught, or screwing it up, just like they screwed up everything else in their lives.

"You need to get really good mother plants and you only take cuttings. You're only going to keep the female plants and throw away the males. Can you tell the difference between a male and female marijuana plant? Put it on your checklist. You need to deal with fungus and mites and all kinds of pests. It's a full-time job, and most guys don't realize how complicated it is."

"How do you know all this stuff?"

"I have a university degree in botany."

"So you know how to grow marijuana?"

"Sure, but like I said, it's not just growing a plant. You need to know all kinds of skills. You have to install electric wiring, fans, ozonators [an apparatus for converting oxygen into ozone], reflectors, and water-pumping systems. You need to set up your thousand-watt halide lights with timers so that the plants have a set period of darkness that changes as they grow. You need to figure out a cover story so that the electric company and the cops don't start wondering why your little warehouse is chewing up enough electricity to light a football stadium."

Well, I would never get involved in something like that. But I found it darned interesting—just like those other guys talking about sexual techniques. When the radio started breaking up, I wanted to turn my truck around and follow this botanist guy so that I could hear the rest of the lecture.

You Think That's Funny?

The radio is your main companion on these long drives, but that can be a mixed blessing. Some of the drivers get a little bit silly after a while. Everybody has a different notion of what makes a funny story. There were these two young guys who used to fool around on the radio, but they were not funny. Doing animal sounds, acting like idiots. I think they needed to change their medication. It was so obnoxious I had to turn the radio off.

People tell me that I have a sense of humor, and I like to think that I can tell a good story. So I'll do my best to entertain the other drivers with a tale or two when things get slow. But I happen to know that certain people do not find me amusing. I'm sure that more than one driver would like to invite me outside and tell me why he doesn't think I'm so darned funny. But I never get to hear their opinions because I'm big and I'm grumpy. You can get away with a lot when you're big and grumpy.

There were these four young drivers who used to be very entertaining. These guys were *funny*. They weren't big and tough and funny. They were just funny. They made up a comedy radio show, complete with commercials, songs, guest stars, and what have you. They could do great accents, and one of them would impersonate a guest star like Guy Lafleur or some other famous athlete or politician. It was really, really entertaining. I would kill myself laughing. If I heard that they were on the radio I would be searching every channel to find them. I didn't recognize all the accents they were doing, but I guess some of them were supposed to be truckers working on the ice road, and I guess some of the guys they were imitating were not amused.

One night one of these funny young guys was sitting at the edge of a lake, waiting for the message on the radio that it was his turn to cross the ice, when another truck pulled up behind him. The driver of the other truck was one of the guys they were mimicking. Well, he got out of his truck and walked over to this young guy's vehicle. Our young comedian must have watched him coming in the rearview mirror. Oh, boy . . . this guy was big. And he was ugly. And he hadn't bathed in a month. He jerked open the door of the truck and pulled that young fella out of the cab and threatened his life right there. Told him he was polluting the airways and to keep his damn idiotic jabber to himself. And that was the end of their radio show.

I was disappointed. You need funny stuff to break up the monotony. These young guys made the miles go by easier. But I guess this big, ugly guy, he thought he was the head of the Radio Television and Telecommunications Commission, and took them off the air.

Religion

They say that you're never supposed to talk about politics or religion at a dinner party. That's not true on the ice road. The more touchy the subject, the more the truckers want to talk about it.

I don't jam my religious faith down anyone's throat, but it's a major part of my life, so I'm not likely to talk very long before the subject comes up. I like philosophy and I like debating with people about interesting ideas, and what could be more interesting than the idea of God? I'm not reluctant to talk to nonbelievers, and if they have really thought about God and decided that he doesn't exist, I respect their opinion. All I'm saying is, Keep an open mind. If you're going to have opinions, you have to have to start off with an open mind.

Keep a healthy respect for doubt. The most dangerous thing you can have is certainty about your own opinions. You have to do your research and be honest about considering the possibility that you might be wrong. If you can't argue against your own beliefs as well as you could argue for them, you're in a lot of trouble, because it means you haven't reviewed the evidence. We all know a hell of a lot less than we think we know. Anyone who thinks that he understands how the world works is deluded.

I've had times when I was almost out of gas, out there on a deserted road in the middle of the night, and I prayed to God to help me, and sure enough, something always happened. My parents and grandparents brought me up a Christian and a Roman Catholic. I heard many stories as a child about God and prayer bringing my family through Siberian concentration camps, the war, and general hard times. They taught me to pray. After leaving home as a teen, I stopped going to church but I came back when I was in my twenties and had a young family. Initially I believed because I had faith in what I was told. As I grew older, I experienced and saw God work in my life and in others'.

I believe in God for simple reasons—I've seen how He can change things in a person's life. I know alcoholics who tried every possible tactic for quitting drinking. And nothing worked until they got down on their knees and asked God to help them. Just ask God for help and your life will change. But don't take my word for it. Talk to some people whose lives have been saved by a simple leap of faith, then ask yourself, "What's the harm in trying it?"

And it doesn't even have to be big problems like addiction. Suppose you're an old person and you're afraid of falling down and breaking your bones. Just put your hands together and say a prayer and ask God to help you and right away you'll notice a difference. You'll find yourself catching your balance just when you were going to fall. Try it. You might be surprised.

And of course some people look at the way I live, cussing and carrying on, and say, "If you believe in God, how can you swear like that?" Well, it's part of my culture. People have a certain way of talking in Paris and we have a certain way of talking in the North. I don't believe swearing makes you a bad person. I have a TRUCKING FOR JESUS sticker on the door of my truck and I do volunteer work in prisons and hospitals. I figure that makes up for a few cuss words. I believe that God can see deep inside your heart. He doesn't sweat the small stuff.

One time I started talking to this other trucker about religion. He was a Mennonite, a grain farmer from northern Saskatchewan, and I guess he didn't go to church very often. I told him, "You're older now and you've got a family, you've got to start thinking about making your peace with God." He had his views and I had mine, and I guess the Mennonites don't have much use for the Catholic religion, but we had a very good talk as we rolled along. We talked religion for six solid hours, all the way from Lockhart to Yellowknife, and I don't think we changed each other's minds in any way, but it was respectful and interesting.

That was years ago, but sometimes I'll run into a trucker who will remind me of that conversation. He'll say, "You know, I once listened to you and some other guy talking religion for six solid hours. And I never placed much faith in the church, but that sure was an interesting conversation. And it made me reconsider my opinion about religion."

That shows you that you never know—someone could be watching you, listening to you. It's not necessarily the big things that we do in life that influence other people. Sometimes it's the small things you don't even notice yourself. I've seen that happen so many times. Every day you get out of bed and go into the world, and you're like a stone hitting the surface of the water. The ripples go out in big circles, but the stone is unaware of them. So many times people have come up to me and told me about something I did that I don't even remember. I've picked up hitchhikers who sent me letters years later from Europe or Australia, telling me how much they enjoyed spending the afternoon swapping stories in my vehicle. But I pick up hitchhikers all the time. Hundreds of them over the course of my life. And I swear I can't remember one from the other.

I remember once I was doing some work out behind the Yellowknife jail. I was doing some clean-up work with a track loader. It had street pads on it and it's early winter, wet snow, and I was in a rush to go somewhere. I was trying to drive up on the back of this trailer and it would slide down off the ramp. I tried and tried and I was getting nowhere. I must have done this for half an hour. If it was summer it would have taken two minutes. So I felt like swearing and yelling but I just kept at it and finally I got it in the trailer. Then a year later this guy comes up to me in the bar and says, "You really impress me. You are the most patient guy I've ever seen. I watched you the whole time you were wrestling with that thing."

"I didn't see you."

"I was in jail."

"Overnight?"

"No, I was in for quite a while. And watching you helped me figure out how I was going to do my time without going crazy. You taught me a little bit about patience."

Curtis Debogorski

My dad could teach us all a thing or two about patience. About five years ago in late August me, Alex Jr., Nelson, Andrew, Dominic, and my dad took off into the Nahanni mountains to Little Doctor Lake, a serene lake between a mountain gorge in one of the most beautiful and rugged parts of our country. Good family friends, Lynn and Liz Fowler, had purchased a cabin from an archaeologist in the early eighties and renovated it to make it a home away from home, with all of the creature comforts to make one's stay very comfortable. Before leaving for the trip Lynn left us with a two-page document to review that provided a history of the area, the best fishing spots, the inclement weather warnings, and strict instructions to leave the place exactly how we found it—neat and tidy. One of the final comments revolved around a rifle that Lynn had at the cabin that could be used in the event that a wandering grizzly or black bear found us while on a hike or around the camp. Lynn's note explained that the rifle was an old family heirloom and meant a great deal to him and he would prefer if we brought our own and only used his as a last resort. I made at least three stern speeches to my younger brothers to ensure the camp was spotless after our stay and that we treat everything like it was our very own.

So after arriving at the camp and settling in, we decided that we would take the two canoes and make our way across the lake to where Lynn had said dry mountain streambeds would take us to the crest of one of the mountains for some inspiring views. Dad warned me immediately that he is like a scared cat around water and that the canoe was a risky mode of transport. Being the oldest boy and figuring I had the best chance of saving the "old man" if he was to go under, I put the pressure on. After a short man-or-mouse challenge, we grabbed the sacred gun as protection, and he caved in and jumped in the front of the canoe. About twenty feet offshore, Dad gets a scare as he shifts left and I shift right. The canoe teeters as we both jostle to set the course straight. Unfortunately while trying to correct the canoe—and with dad weighing at least 50 pounds more than me—the weight displacement became too great and we tipped on our side with a great splash. Out of the boat went the fishing tackle, our backpacks, and "Oh shit! The damn gun!"

The first order of business was to make sure we didn't go down, as the water was frigid. We both struggled to turn the canoe over and make our way back to shore to reassess the situation. As always in times of crisis Dad was calm and collected as my blood pressure began to rise thinking of the "golden gun." Once we were on solid ground, I realized the gun was gone. Nelson, the third-oldest boy, decided to venture back out into the water to determine the depth where we went down. He dove down a few feet and came back up hyperventilating from the sheer cold. "It's gotta be fifty feet deep!" he exclaimed. Distraught, and after many swear words and accusations about who caused the canoe to tip, we brainstormed and scoured the camp looking for anything to help us salvage the missing gun. After a short search I came from the shed with a fish stringer. Dad waded out into the water a few feet while Nelson outfitted himself in a dry suit that looked two sizes too small and put his future as a fertile father in jeopardy. For the next two hours Dad would calmly throw the stringer out 20 feet offshore, hoping he would somehow snag the gun and bring it back to the surface. After about an hour of watching him toss the rope and Nelson dive within minutes of hypothermia, the other boys and I started to say, "It's a lost cause, let's just get back out there and enjoy the rest of the day!" Dad, being persistent and patient, said, "You guys go ahead. I'll stay back and try and find this damn thing."

We slowly packed up again to head to the dry riverbeds when Dad exclaimed, "I've got something!" Nelson waded out to where the rope was in the water and dove down. Seconds later he emerged victoriously clutching the gun high above his head with both arms outstretched. With a war cry he screamed, "I've got it!" We immediately cheered and high-fived while Dad calmly pulled the rope in and mumbled something about patience with a crooked smirk. We then happily went about our day. Dad went back to the cabin, cleaned the gun methodically, and shot it to ensure it was fully functioning. To this day Lynn is unaware of this tale, and what better way to bring it to light than in Dad's first book!

Caution: Wolverine Xing

So after a long night of driving the sun finally comes up.

You get these incredible sunrises in the North—first comes this glow of pink and mauve in the east, then a fiery orange like the open door of a furnace. Sunlight floods across the ice and jagged snow, throwing purple shadows. Through February and March the days get longer quickly. The shades of the pastel colors change every day because of the changing of the sun's angle.

Then the animals start stirring. You felt as if you were alone all night long, but now you realize you're sharing this frigid landscape with all kinds of interesting wild creatures.

One of the weirdest animals we have up here is the wolverine.

From the name, you might think they are related to the wolf, but they are not. They're just low-slung little critters, not much bigger than a badger or a little dog. They're actually related to weasels. But man, they are mean. There is no animal in the North as ferocious and fearless as a wolverine. They're like our own version of that Tasmanian Devil in the cartoons. They will follow a trapper for days, ruining his trap sets, defecating on his campfires, and destroying every animal he catches. They just seem to hate people, and everything else, for that matter. They'll tear a hole in the roof of a trapline cabin and wreck the place just to be spiteful. And there are lots of authenticated accounts of them driving a grizzly bear away from its kill.

I'll see a wolverine sometimes when I'm on the ice roads. The hunters will shoot a caribou and leave the gut pile beside the road. Then a wolverine will come along and feed on it. Every time a truck comes by, the wolverine gets more pissed off. Then finally he loses it. He just goes ballistic. When you're bearing down on him in the truck you will see him crouch down snarling as the truck approaches. Then he'll just blow a head gasket as you go past. He's just like some insane little varmint in a cartoon. You'll see him in the rearview mirror, chasing this fifty-ton truck, snapping at the mud flaps.

When you're driving the ice road, you have to be very careful that you don't run over an animal. There are very strict laws against that, and we have to fill out a report if it happens. The environmental restrictions on ice road trucking are incredibly strict, much more so than they are for trucking in the South. Guys used to stand and pee off the running boards while the truck was rolling along. Some of them of course would slip on the ice and fall off the truck and then the truck would be driving along with nobody in it! On more than one occasion I've heard of a truck puttering down the road by itself with some frustrated truck driver running behind like crazy trying to catch up with it. But now you're not allowed to pee on the snowbank because of the environmental rules. The theory is, some wolf or fox will be attracted to the spot. He's going to think some creature has invaded his territory, and while he's standing there sniffing at the yellow snow a truck is going to come along and run over him. I know it sounds a little ludicrous, but it just shows how fussy they are about keeping the landscape absolutely clean. So now a lot of guys will pee in a bottle so they don't get in trouble for hitting an animal. You wouldn't want to hit one of these animals anyway. Some of them are enormous. The moose here are the biggest moose in the world. Farther north, you get into polar bears and grizzlies.

When you drive from Fort Providence up to Yellowknife you'll see these warning signs beside the road with buffalo on them. I'm not kidding. Most southerners think that buffalo were all wiped out during the 1800s on the Great Plains. But we still have thousands of wild buffalo up here. Keep your eyes peeled and you'll see them standing in the woods as you go by. Lots of times you come around a corner and they'll be standing right in the middle of the road. Sometimes they'll run when they see a vehicle; sometimes they'll stand there and glare at you. It's very difficult to predict what a wild buffalo is going to do. And since a bull weighs over two thousand pounds, you want to be very careful when you're driving at night.

Our wolves are big, too. I guess it has something to do with heat efficiency. Big animals don't lose their body heat as quickly as small animals. Arctic wolves have long legs, and when you see one crossing the ice road up ahead of the truck, they're so big you sometimes mistake them for a caribou.

My friend Dave Smith and I are both curmudgeonly. We've lived in Yellowknife over thirty years and on occasion have shared the same shack in the bush, drank the same frozen beer, and have been wakened in the morning by the same bears. Dave does a lot of freighting work with his boat on Great Slave Lake and he has a wolfskin on the back of his couch at his home in Yellowknife. Pure white, with beautiful fur about four inches thick. He got it from a trapper who told him it was the biggest wolf he'd ever caught. If you measure this wolf it's eight feet from the tip of the nose to the base of the tail. Imagine going out for a walk one day and meeting an animal that size face-to-face.

You'll see lots of caribou crossing the roads, especially the Tibbit to Contwoyto Winter Road. Sometimes you'll see wolves before you see the caribou. If you see wolves that means there's caribou around. The wolves are always following the caribou and picking them off. Of course, when you get the caribou carcasses you will get foxes, wolverines, ravens, and eagles cleaning them up. The hunters come along and shoot a few caribou and leave the gut piles. That attracts the birds and the animals.

When you're driving along you can see those ravens from a long way off. You'll see these black shapes sitting on the snow, and that means there's a caribou down. Where there's the remains of a caribou, you're going to see wildlife. Might be a fox, or even a wolf. Pure white, like a ghost—you won't see him unless you look real hard and then all of a sudden he's just standing there.

I like telling people about the giant rabbits we have up here. They're properly called Arctic hares. These things are a lot bigger than most big rabbits. How big are they? Well, one time I was sleeping behind the wheel. I hear a noise and I turn my head and there's one of them Arctic hares looking right in the side window. Darn ears were sticking up over the door handle of the truck. This rabbit was almost as tall as a man in a bunny suit. Okay, maybe that's a bit of an exaggeration, but these rabbits get big.

The town of Yellowknife is full of ravens. They're always getting into mischief. They will tease dogs and steal stuff. They are a lot like people in some ways. They are sociable, they never stop talking, and they are always working the angles, so they get along real well in an urban setting.

You have to be careful putting down your tools or your car keys because some raven will come in and snatch them just for fun. The Indians have many stories and legends about ravens, and they regard them as the tricksters of the North. They are looking for a way to tease mankind and steal his food. They say that animals don't have a soul, but I can tell you that they definitely have a sense of humor. You don't have to be an expert on the subject, it's just common sense. If you spend enough time in the North and you watch these animals you can tell that sometimes they're just having fun.

One time I saw a raven swinging on a telephone wire. He would hold on to it with his feet, then cock his head in a goofy kind of way and swing upside down, hanging by his claws. He looked like a toy up there, swinging back and forth and using his wings to get back upright again. I guess he was enjoying himself after a good meal, just playing like a kid in a schoolyard. They are also really good imitators. If you're out in the bush, banging nails or splitting wood or running a power tool, you will sometimes hear someone else working after you stop. You look around, thinking, *What the heck, is someone else chopping wood out here?* Then you look in a tree and see it's just a raven making chopping sounds, having some fun with you.

I sometimes play a joke on them, too. Driving down the ice road, I'll put a sandwich on my dashboard. A raven will go flying past, he'll spot that sandwich, and he'll come in for a landing on the hood of my truck. As soon as his buddies see him, they'll come zooming in to see what's going on. Before you know it I'll have two or three ravens skidding around on the hood of the truck, cocking their heads this way and that because they can only see properly out of one eye at a time, pecking the windshield and trying to figure out how they are going to get that sandwich. It's pretty comical. They are smart birds and they know there's no point in pecking at window glass. But they just can't bring themselves to fly away without trying to get that sandwich.

You can't actually feed them, though. The rule book states it in black and white: "Feeding wildlife while operating/travelling on or near the Winter Road is strictly prohibited."

I've never gotten in trouble for hitting an animal. And that's good, because I like animals and they make a long drive way more interesting. One day I was driving down the ice road and I saw the strangest sight. A whole bunch of little crawly black critters came boiling up over the snowbank and ran onto the road right in front of the truck. I slammed on the brakes thinking, *What the heck is this?*

Well, I'll be darned if it's not a family of otters!

I always thought they lived in the open water, rivers and lakes. But here they are way out in the middle of the ice road, on a bitter winter day, with the air temperature at least thirty degrees below zero. It was Mum and Dad and the kids, about three little ones, and they were pretty darn surprised to see this massive truck coming at them right in the middle of nowhere.

As soon as they saw me, Mum and Dad were concentrating on getting off the road, but the kids weren't too worried. In fact, they weren't worried at all. They looked like they were having a whale of a time, and that's when I realized why they were out here on the ice road. When they plow the ice road they leave these steep snowbanks on both shoulders, and the otters always cross a frozen lake just so they could slide on the snowbanks. The parents were kind of worried about the truck, but the young ones ignored me. They would just run up the snowbank, slide to the bottom on their bellies, and then run back up to do the same thing again. They looked just like a bunch of kids at a toboggan park, and you could tell by their expressions that they weren't going to let a gigantic truck disturb their afternoon of fun.

I had to stop and watch them for a while. Didn't have a camera, but I'll never forget the sight of those animals whooping it up in the snow. They have got to be one of the neatest, funniest animals on the land. I don't know much about dolphins, but I imagine that otters are like a furry four-legged dolphin, with the same sense of humor.

Humor is one of the main things about living in the North. People up here are funny, and they are good storytellers. And it seems like most of the funny stories have an animal in them. There are lots of bear stories, for example. I don't know how many run-ins I've had with bears. And there was always something funny about it.

Like this one time, in the off-season, I was working in a bush camp with some diamond drillers. For some reason diamond drillers always seem to be afraid of bears. So my buddy Dave and I gathered up this bear shit from outside and took it over to the drill shack where they usually ate dinner and put this bear shit on the floor. And then we sprayed it with bug spray to make it look like it was fresh and still damp, and then sprinkled it with bread crumbs to make it look like he was eating that. Then we kicked over a few pails and made a little bit of a mess the same way that a bear might knock things down, and then off we went.

One of these drillers was pretty experienced in the bush, so he wasn't too concerned. In fact, he was such a cool customer that he never even mentioned it. But this other guy, this rookie, he was scared silly. He couldn't stop talking about it: "Oh, man, this bear must be really dangerous, walking right into the cook shack like he did. What are we going to do about this bear? I'm not getting paid to fight bears," and so on. It was his main subject of conversation.

And of course Dave and I were having trouble keeping control of ourselves because it was so funny. We'd be sitting at dinner listening to this city boy going on and on about this big, dangerous bear that was going to pull us out of our sleeping bags and rip us apart and we'd practically blow food out our noses trying not to laugh.

Another time, I was in this drilling camp by myself and this one bear would come and visit me. The cabin door opened to the inside, and every night around one in the morning, when I was lying asleep in bed, the door would swing open and this bear would look inside at me. I don't know how that woke me up, but I would open my eyes and get a hell of a start because this bear would be looking at me. I wasn't too worried that it was going to eat me, but it makes it hard to sleep when you're thinking that at any moment a bear might walk in.

So this got to be quite annoying, and one night when the bear showed up I went outside and yelled at it. I had this little Defender 12-gauge shotgun—have you ever seen one? They're a neat little gun and they'll knock a door off the hinges. I shout, "Hey," to the bear. And it just looks at me. It's turning its head back and forth and you can just tell by its expression that it doesn't know what I am. I guess it's never seen a man before. I aim the gun at the ground next to the bear and I fire a slug into the gravel at its feet. *Kaboom!* Stones and earth go flying and that bear jumps three feet in the air. It takes off running and I fire another shot into the sand right under its heels to give it a good send-off.

Later on, the rest of the crew shows up, and of course when you have workers, you have food, and when you have food you get bears. Despite what anyone tells you about "bearproofing" your campsite, you simply cannot live in an area for any length of time without attracting bears. Even if you're out on the land and you pee on the ground, animals will come and investigate that spot. So naturally, we started getting bears. And the drillers were terrified. These bears would come around the cook tent and oh, boy, you could hear everyone yelling and banging pans, trying to scare them away.

I don't know why, but I would just stamp my foot and they would take off running like they had seen the devil. I told the cook that it must have been my body odor. They were all bathing with Herbal Essence, and I smelled like a mountain man. But I don't know the real reason. Maybe the word got out or something. That one bear must have told the other ones: "Stay away from that big guy. He has a bad temper."

An Unusual Hitchhiker

One time I was driving down the road with a buddy and I saw this eagle sitting up ahead on the side of the road. You'll often see them sitting on a dead animal, so the eagle itself wasn't unusual. It was just the way he was sitting. You know how sometimes you can look at an animal and just tell that there's something wrong with it? I don't know if this thing had been hit by a vehicle, but I could tell that something wasn't right.

I got out and walked over to the eagle. As soon as he saw me coming he reared back on his tail and spread his wings out like a tripod and extended his claws and started clicking his beak at me. I guess that's how they defend themselves. I had a light windbreaker on, so I took it off and threw it over the eagle and picked him up. He was big and heavy. I mean, he was as big as a barnyard turkey. I told my friend Ian to drive, and I climbed in with his eagle on my lap. "What are we going to do with it?" my buddy said.

"I have no idea but there must be a place that takes injured eagles."

So we were driving down the road and I had this big damn bird on my lap and his claws were sitting right on my crotch. His claws were about the size of my hands, and that made me wonder if maybe I was making an error in judgment. If this bird grabbed me by the balls I would be in serious trouble. So I said to Ian, "If this son of a bitch goes crazy on me, jam on the brakes and I'm going to wring his neck and throw him out the window."

Having grown up on a farm, I know how to kill a bird real quick, and I really didn't like the idea of those big claws sitting about an inch away from the family jewels! Of course, I didn't want to scare him, but every time we hit a bump I could feel his claws tense up a little bit and all kinds of interesting thoughts were going through my mind about what I was going to do if he just suddenly grabbed me. Finally I said, "Let's take him to the RCMP. They'll know what to do with him."

So we survived the journey down the road and we got to Fort Providence and went into the little police detachment there. And of course the constable there was about twenty-one years old and he didn't have a clue what he was supposed to do with this eagle. It just showed you how we expect the police to be able to fix any kind of problem. I mean, here's this young cop and he knows even less than we do. He said, "What do you expect me to do with it?"

"I don't know; you're the cop."

"But nobody ever brought me an eagle before."

"Well, all I know is, these things are protected by law and that means you're in charge of protecting it."

"Okay, bring it in here."

He had a doggie cage in the back, a cage for bad dogs, and he put it in there. This poor eagle, now he's in jail. Anyway, we left, but I read about that bird a week later. That young cop drove that eagle for two hundred miles to Yellowknife and gave it to a vet, who rehabilitated it and put it back in the wild. That young policeman was a little aggravated when we dumped that eagle on him, but you could tell from that newspaper story that he got into the spirit of the rescue. It was probably the most interesting thing he did all month.

The Mouse That Wrecked a Car

Speaking of funny animal stories, I sometimes entertain the truckers with the story of the time that a mouse wrecked my Mark III Lincoln.

It all started with this time that my son Curtis and I took a driving trip to Victoria. There was a battleship in the harbor and I wanted to have a look at it. We were walking across the street and he threw a tantrum right in the middle of the cross-walk. He was about five years old. He laid down right in the road and the thought crossed my mind that if I could pack him in a box I would just send him as cargo direct home to Yellowknife.

Then we went to visit my cousin Justina, whose daughter Simone is just as pretty as a picture. I think her dad was

Jamaican and played the trumpet in a reggae band. She had two pet white mice, and her mom offered them to Curtis as a present.

They had a cage, so we took these white mice with us. As we were driving from Vancouver back to Yellowknife, well, one of these dang mice got loose in the car, and the only time it would come out was when you were driving. He'd come out and sit on your knee, but as soon as you'd stop, he would disappear. I'd leave food and water for the mouse because I didn't want it to die inside the seat and rot and stink up the car.

One day my sister wanted to borrow the car and see her boyfriend in Fort Rae, so I gave her the Lincoln and off she went. Well, on the way back from seeing her boyfriend, the mouse came out and sat on her knee. She grabbed the mouse but while she and the mouse were wrassling around, she forgot to pay attention to the road. She flipped the car and ended up hanging upside down over deep water.

She crawled out of there with the mouse in her hand, brought the mouse home, and put it in the cage with the other one. The car was a write-off.

Now she had to go to the police station, where she was working as a secretary. Normally she's on one side of the desk, but now she's on the other. She's the one giving the statement, so she's all stressed out. She says to me, "What am I going to tell the RCMP? I work for them!"

I said, "Tell them the truth. You don't tell them the whole truth. You don't have to tell them where the mouse came from. You don't have to tell them what color the mouse was, unless they ask, and believe me, they're not going to ask you what color the mouse was. Tell them a mouse ran up your leg, that's all you have to say."

I can see that she doesn't like the sound of this.

So I say to her, "Okay, did the mouse run up your leg or did it not run up your leg?"

"The mouse ran up my leg."

"Just friggin' tell them that."

She nods.

"And don't friggin' tell them it was white!"

So she goes in to make the statement and she's all nervous.

The cop sits down and gets out a piece of paper for her to make her statement. He gives her this stone-faced look and says, "Tell me what happened."

"A mouse ran up my leg."

"I beg your pardon?"

"Well, I was driving down the highway and this mouse ran up my leg and I lost control of the vehicle."

The cop bursts out laughing. He can't stop laughing. Everybody in the police station is looking at him. You can see that everyone is wondering what's so funny. My sister is trying to get the situation under control by maintaining a dead serious face and telling him more details of the story—like how she felt something on her leg and looked down and the mouse was sitting on her knee—but every time she adds another detail to the story, he laughs even harder. Finally he gets control of himself. "Then what happened?"

"Well, I lost control, and the car flipped over and rolled into the ditch and ended up half submerged in deep water."

Now he's laughing so hard he's got tears rolling down his face. "Sorry about that," he finally says after he gets control of himself. "Sign it right at the bottom with the date and the time."

The cop went down and told everyone else in the police detachment, and within an hour anybody who had anything to do with the Northwest Territories government heard about it. For the next two weeks, everywhere she went, people burst out laughing. "A mouse ran up your leg and you lost control of the vehicle?"

"Yes, that's the truth."

She didn't tell them the mouse was white. And she didn't tell them that when she climbed out of the wreck she had the little bugger in her hand. That would have really got them howling.

The Diamond Mine

So these stories help to pass the miles.

And eventually, after hauling a massive load of fuel, power-generating equipment, or prefabricated buildings, we'll get to the end of the road and the diamond mine will come into sight.

At the mine site, this is what you see—gigantic earth movers about the size of an apartment building going eight hundred feet down into the mine to scoop up tons of this broken rock. It's pretty shocking if you've never seen it before, and these mines are located in some of the most beautiful wilderness areas you've ever seen. Environmentalists are always complaining about mining development in the North, and if you stood there looking at an open-pit mine you might understandably feel a bit pissed off.

But it's all temporary. I've lived up here now for most of my life, and I've seen a lot of these mining operations come and go. The fact is, today's mining camp is about the cleanest form of development you are ever going to find anywhere. It's much cleaner than your average farm or golf course. A mine is temporary. It's only going to be here for twenty or thirty years, which adds up to about two or three seconds in the history of this land. Even the ice road is temporary. Spring comes along and you would never even know that big trucks were rolling along these lakes. They are very strict about ensuring that we don't leave any lasting marks on the landscape. We are not allowed to spill a single drop of oil from our trucks or there is hell to pay. Mining is a much cleaner activity than almost anything they do in the urbanized South.

When a drilling camp is finished, the company has to clean up everything and put that site back into pristine condition. I worked on these sites, and I can tell you that when they are gone you wouldn't even know there was ever any activity there. If they wanted to really protect the environment they would get rid of some towns and cities and make all these armchair environmentalists go out and work in mining camps in the bush. That would be good for a few chuckles.

So you've got this enormous hole in the ground and these giant trucks getting loaded with granite and kimberlite, which they haul to the top, where it is taken to a processing plant and run through crushing machines to separate the diamonds. The processing machines are all automated, and security is real tight. It's like a James Bond movie, cameras and guards and heavy surveillance. You work in there, you're not even allowed to pick something up off the floor. In fact, the average person can't go anywhere near the diamond processing plant. It's all locked down and seriously out of bounds.

When you're making truck runs into and out of these mines the security can be pretty heavy-handed. I guess you might think it's comical if you have a sense of humor. I'm a fairly good-natured guy and I'll put up with a lot of things, but at times I do find that the security gets to be a little ridiculous. So we'll do things to tease the security guards and get each other in trouble. Like we'll tell the security guard that Jay Westgard is actually only fifteen and doesn't have a driver's license. And he looks so young and they'll make him show his driver's license sometimes, and that's always good for a laugh.

You will get these security guards crawling through our trucks, looking to see if we're stealing diamonds, and that can be irritating, too. We live in the trucks for two months of the year, and they get in there with snow on their feet and get slush all over everything. They'll get in the bunk and they'll start lifting up pillows, digging through your personal stuff. We sign a release form that allows them to search your truck. And they do it.

So you have to get used to that. I don't have anything to hide, but it's the principle. I remember this one security lady who would climb into my truck and go through everything. Makes you feel like you're ten years old again, getting in trouble with the teacher. One day I was walking past the front of my truck and I saw her searching through my private stuff, opening my thermos even. She stuck her nose in my thermos, smelled it, and gave it a shake to see if I had hidden any diamonds in it.

So I'm outside thinking, *Hey, it's cold and everybody's got a runny nose and this is kind of bad, you know?* Some stranger's sticking her runny nose in my thermos. I don't know if she's checking for booze or whatever, but I saw her do that to a few guys.

This one day, we were in the dispatch shack, and I was talking to the other guys. This security officer was back there doing all her paperwork and listening in, so I said, "My wife won't allow me to pee outside when it's twenty below. She doesn't want me to damage the family jewels. So I've got to pee in my thermos."

A couple years later I ran into this lady.

She said, "Do you remember me?"

"You were security on the mine up there, weren't you?"

"Yes, I was. And I just want to tell you that I heard you that day."

"Which day was that?"

"The day that you said you peed in your thermos."

I laughed and told her I was just having some fun with her. She said, "I never stuck my nose in a thermos again."

It's Never Safe to Relax

Mining camps are like small towns. They've got nice lunchrooms, showers, movies, and places to sleep. But you know me, always chasing a buck. When I married my wife I swore I would work myself to death for her and the kids. But Polacks are so tough that it takes forty or fifty years' worth of hard labor to kill one of us.

So I don't dawdle at the mining camp. I just refill my thermos and my fuel tanks and head south—I've got cats to kill and contracts to fill. But nothing is easy in this business, and sometimes the weather can turn nasty in five minutes. The landscape is so flat up here that if it starts to snow and the wind starts to blow, the visibility can drop down to zero during that time it takes you to zip up your fly and wash your hands. Sometimes you're all excited about turning her around and heading home, and then the weather closes down on top of the mining camp and you realize you're not going anywhere. Pretty soon the yard is full of idling trucks and everybody is suddenly pissed off because they're sitting around doing nothing and they have no idea when the dispatcher is going to give them the clearance to go.

We've got this dispatcher named Grumpy Old Alec. It seems like he's always peeved off, and he has a memory like an elephant. When he's dispatching he's basically God. Let's say that we get weathered in at the Lockart Lake Camp along with two hundred other trucks. By the time we get parked there's a hundred trucks in front of us, and when the weather clears enough Alec starts letting four trucks go every half hour, which adds up to eight per hour. So we are looking at twelve to twenty hours before we're getting out of here. There's nothing to do, you're burning time, you can't really go and hang around in the lunchroom or you might lose your place, so you just sit there waiting and waiting, and everybody is cranky as hell.

Sometimes Alec will send them out in bigger groups, depending on how early it is in the season and what kind of shape the ice is in. They can't have too many trucks going out onto the ice at the same time. It's just asking for a disaster. So of course everybody's trying to jockey for position, find some kind of excuse why they should get out first. Everybody is bugging Alec and he's getting pretty irritated. "Don't bother me! I'll let you know when you can go."

Me and Roman aren't saying a thing. Alec knows we're out here, and he knows we're keeping our mouths shut. So the weather starts to clear and the wind dies down. The storm is blowing itself out—but even with the wind dying down, you've got to wait for the plows to open the road, which takes another five or six hours. The odd guy is still in the camp eating, drinking, shooting the breeze, but the rest of us serious guys are in our trucks, fidgeting, jockeying for position, trying to figure out how we're going to squeeze our way out ahead of the rest of the pack.

Pretty soon Alec calls me and Roman. "Okay, go."

He's put us right in the front of the list! So we jump in our trucks and take off. "Thank you, sir."

Well, right away there's a whole big kerfuffle from the other drivers. All kinds of other guys in their trucks are yelling at Alec on the two-way radio: "Why'd you let them go?"

As we hit the road, a couple of other trucks pull right in behind us. And Alec's watching this whole performance and he comes on the radio: "You guys turn around and come back or you're fired."

"Well, what about them?"

"Never mind about them. You guys line up and wait your turn. Security will lead you out."

So off we go. The other trucks have to go back, line up behind the security pickup. Maybe half an hour later security will let them go. These truckers are like a bunch of bulls. One of the truckers will jockey in front of the other one and then the whole herd gets worked up and the next thing you know you've got a stampede. A hundred trucks racing out onto the ice all at the same time. Can you imagine the potential for disaster? Can you imagine that lake suddenly breaking like a big piece of plate glass with all those trucks on it?

Man, it would make front-page news all around the world.

So that is Alec for you. He will use me and Roman to get back at all these other guys who had been bugging him for a day. The lesson is, don't mess with the dispatcher. It might be annoying to sit and wait for the dispatcher to call your name, but it's better to be waiting inside the cab of an idling truck than to be lying upside down on the bottom of the lake.

So eventually the dispatcher will give us clearance to go and we head south, the truck riding a little rougher now because we're empty. The trucks always ride a little smoother when they are fully loaded. When they're empty, they just bounce like a paint shaker. I remember about eight years ago, the ice road was really bad. The north end of MacKay Lake had holes a foot deep everywhere. It was just like it had been bombed. You'd get a little snow blowing across the road and you couldn't see and you'd be hitting those holes and pounding the snot right out of your truck.

Oh, it was terrible. We would slow down, but I mean MacKay Lake at 20 miles an hour is already over three hours long. Slow down to 15 or less and it's four hours long and you'd be holding up the trucks behind you and making them angry, so you'd try to swerve in and out of these holes and you couldn't see anything. You're hitting potholes and banging your head on the ceiling and scaring yourself half to death.

When the road gets that bad, the maintenance crews can't keep up with it by flooding and filling all the holes. So they were building a new lane. They plowed the snow off it to let the cold air get at the ice so that it would thicken up enough to hold loaded trucks. The road's got to be overbuilt so there's no chance somebody's going to go through.

So everybody has to be patient, and you know truckers—they're not the most patient type. Their attitude is, to hell with all that, let's just give her. Along comes this guy named Dog. He's right fed up with bashing his truck on this road and he pulls over into this new road, which is nice and smooth, but still closed. As soon as Dog starts roaring down this nice new road, one of the top superintendents starts following right behind him.

Dog has been around the block a few times. He's kind of ragged. He's a bit of a rabble-rouser. If he could start a union, he would. And he was telling everybody, the hell with it, and he was going to use this new road and if they didn't like it they could, rah, rah, and so on.

All of a sudden this supervisor starts laying into him. "What are you doing on this road?"

Well, the battle was on. Dog said what he was going to do and now he was doing it. Dog wasn't just talk. And you should have heard him lay into the supervisor.

The supervisor says, "Don't you know this road is not ready? You're going to put your truck through the ice."

Dog says, "I don't give a damn if I go through the ice. At least I'll be taking a nice, smooth trip to the bottom of the lake."

They argued and yelled on each other right to the end of the lake. The supervisor said he was going to fire him and Dog said, go ahead and fire me. No matter how much he threatened and shouted, the supervisor simply could not put the fear of the Lord in this character. It was quite entertaining for the rest of us. When they got to the other end of the lake, they both got out and did some more screaming and hollering and cursing. But it all ended in a tie. Dog didn't get fired, and I guess he made his point, because pretty soon that new stretch of road was cleared and we had a nice, smooth ride across MacKay Lake.

On the return trip, the other problem is that everybody wants to speed. They're driving empty trucks. They're not stressing the road so much. What's the problem with giving her a little juice? The temptation to speed is especially bad when the trucks are coming up to the shore. The ice road across the lake is nice and flat, but when you come off the lake the portage road is often pretty steep. That's when things get interesting.

A lot of the drivers speed up before they hit the portage because they're afraid of losing their momentum and getting stuck halfway up the hill. They'll get bogged down and they'll put chains on their drive wheels, then they'll spin the wheels so hard they'll dig a hole a foot deep and even throw the chains off. It makes an awful pothole and the only way to fix it is to fill it with sand and water or snow and water. Then when the thaw starts in the springtime, those holes will melt and you get to find out how strong your suspension is when you hit one of those deep holes with your front wheels. Sometimes you hit them so hard that you can knock your head on the roof of the cab. That's usually when some young driver spins his rig out and blocks the road for two or three hours. Now a winch truck has to come from Timbuktu and meanwhile all the other drivers have to sit and wait. And of course that's when they get on the radio and start cussing out the driver. "Where did you get your license, in a popcorn box?"

I feel like saying, It's an accident, you guys, take a deep breath and relax because there's not a darn thing you can do about it. It never occurs to them that next week it could be them in the same situation.

One time I was crossing Portage 13, which is a stretch of bulldozed road going through some low hills and spruce forest. On the other side of the portage I drove down toward the lake. If you weren't an experienced driver you would have been shocked because the lake looked wide open—bright sun glittering on blue water. But I knew it was actually just a sheet of melted water sitting on top of the ice. We call it "overflow." Sometimes these passages of overflow can make you a little nervous, especially if no one else has driven across them. I've been out on Great Slave Lake, driving a truck all by myself, and come to a long stretch of water that you're pretty sure is just overflow sitting on top of the ice, but of course you can never be a hundred percent certain there's good, hard ice sitting under that water if no one else has been crossing it. It's psychological more than anything. It just doesn't feel too good, driving a truck into a patch of open water. But most of the time you don't worry too much because other trucks are going through the water and you know it's okay. So I just gave her, and hit the ice and drove through the water. When I got to the other side I could see some trucks up ahead. They were sitting crooked on the portage road, maybe a hundred feet up from the lake shore, and right away I get that uneasy feeling—Okay, we've got trouble.

I'm leading a pack of trucks and I tell the guys behind me, Hold off, we've got an accident. They're only a mile or two behind me, so I immediately get on the radio and tell them to hold off and stay on the portage, on dry land. The last thing we need is a bunch of trucks conglomerating in the middle of the lake. In times like this I sometimes take my seat belt off—if this truck breaks through I don't want to be strapped in it! Sometimes I'll even drive with my door cracked open, ready to bail out if I have to.

I jump out of the truck in my shirtsleeves. One truck has slammed into another. The culprit was the southbound truck. It was going too fast. He had to make a right turn coming to the portage. He was sliding, and hit the loaded northbound truck that had stopped to let the southbound truck onto the portage. Since the accident, the portage has been rerouted to make it straighter onto the ice. The northbound truck is a big tanker loaded with diesel fuel, and that fuel is pouring out of a hole in the tank. The tractor of the southbound truck is jammed up against the ruptured tank, and the trucker is trapped inside. This looks bad.

The windshield is smashed, the door is jammed shut, and the guy inside the cab tells me he's too injured to climb out. My biggest concern is fire, but he's hauling a full load, so at least that's better than an empty tank, which is more dangerous because vapor is explosive. I climb up on the rig and tell the driver to relax. "Don't worry, partner, I'm gonna get you out."

I've been in this situation myself—trapped inside a crushed machine, all busted up, with well-meaning but half-crazed rescuers yanking and pulling at me from every direction. I don't want to make it worse for this fella than it already is, so I take a good look at the situation and tell him that I'm going to get him out of the cab and he's going to be okay.

I run back to my truck and grab a big pry bar and some blankets. I climb up on his truck, rip the door off with the pry bar, and start pulling the fella out of the cab. He's a big guy, bigger than me—I'm guessing he's six-six and close to three hundred pounds—so he's a little hard to handle. But I manage to ease him down onto the ice and pull him a safe distance away from the truck. I wrap him in a sleeping bag and get a few pillows under his head. First I don't want him to burn to death, and now I don't want him to freeze!

Ice road security arrives, and they call for a medevac helicopter from Yellowknife. Good luck. That's going to take a while. They have to go through all this red tape before the helicopter can take off—they need to load up the medical equipment and put together the rescue team, so the poor guy lying on the ice is going to have to wait two and a half hours for the chopper. The main concern, after I drag him a safe distance from the truck, is the fuel tanker. It's a got a hole in it about an inch across and diesel fuel is streaming out of it like from a hose. If all that fuel pooling up on the ground catches fire, it's going to set off the tanker and we're going to have a blaze that'll roast everything within a quarter mile.

So I run to my truck and get a sledgehammer, run back to the tanker, and start hammering on that hole, trying to close it up. You wouldn't want to be doing this with gasoline, of course—one spark and you're going to cause a fuel air explosion that'll throw a fireball a hundred feet into the sky—but it's twenty below zero and it's diesel fuel, so I'm hoping I can get away with it. The tanker is only thirty feet from the lake shore, and once the diesel fuel gets onto the ice we're looking at a major environmental cleanup. Once I get the hole closed up with the sledgehammer I get to work building a makeshift boom around the pool of diesel fuel. The chopper finally arrives, we load the man, and off he goes to the hospital. An empty tanker truck arrives and pumps out the leaky tanker. After that's all done with, they let us proceed with our trip. So I summon the other boys in the convoy and we carry on.

At the end of the year they go over the trucking season and figure out what went right and what went wrong, and they give out cash prizes to truckers as safety awards. For my part in the rescue I got five hundred dollars in Canadian Tire money, which are coupons issued by Canadian Tire to buy their products.

I kind of laughed at that. You don't do these things for a reward. And if you did, you'd be saying, *Wait a minute, that's all I get for saving a guy's life and preventing an environmental cleanup that would have cost a million dollars?*

7

HOLLYWOOD COMES TO TOWN

"Throw yourself into it and do the best
job possible."

I guess some of these stories about the drama and danger of driving heavy trucks on thin ice caught the attention of the TV people in Hollywood. The U.S. cable channel HISTORY™ decided they wanted to find out more about these crazy truck drivers who wrestle trucks over frozen lakes through some of the harshest conditions on the planet. So the network sent a TV crew up to Yellowknife to see what they could find out about the ice road trucking business.

It wasn't the first time that TV producers wanted to film the ice roads. It seemed like every year we had a Japanese or German or English crew come up here to shoot footage, and

I enjoyed telling them about the stuff we have to deal with on the ice roads.

Dawn Fitzgerald

I'm a television producer.

Most television shows start off with an idea. Whether it's a drama or a documentary, the creator of the show will come up with some characters and a situation and then try to sell the concept to a network. In this case, it worked backward—the HISTORY™ channel said, "We want to do a show about ice road trucking. Go out and find the characters."

So we were under a certain amount of pressure to find some good story lines and interesting people. We went up to Yellowknife knowing absolutely nothing about the North and even less about ice road trucking. It was Halloween, cold and stormy, and we turned Yellowknife upside down, talking to people and trying to find characters who might be effective on a television show. No matter where we went we heard the same story: "You have to meet Alex Debogorski."

The trouble was, we couldn't find him. He was out on Great Slave Lake somewhere. It was hard to believe that anyone would be out on that lake at that time of year. It's like an ocean—giant waves, blowing snow. But we didn't have any choice but to wait. It's expensive being on the road. We were going through a lot of money for meals and hotel rooms, but it was pretty obvious that we couldn't leave without talking to him. At the tail end, that was mainly what we were doing in Yellowknife—killing time and waiting for Alex.

One time, for example, I walked into the dispatch office and there was this big camera set up in there and these rather small Japanese people behind it. Their English wasn't very good, but they pointed the camera at me and made me understand that they wanted me to say something about the different dangers you face up here in the wilderness of the North. Well, I told them that one of the things that I was most concerned about was GMOs—genetically modified organisms.

I said, "I'm sure you've heard about genetically modified grain and livestock and other controversial stuff, but we have weird stuff affecting our environment up here in the North you probably haven't heard about."

Oh, they liked the sound of that. Controversy! The environment! They were smiling now and nodding for me to continue.

"Well, one of the big problems we have up here is with alien species like zebra mussels. They latch onto the bottom of a ship and it's very difficult and expensive to remove them."

I was making up this story as I went along, and having some fun with it. As I have mentioned, my mother was an artistic woman, and thanks to her I've got a poetic streak in me—nothing I like more than telling a good story. You just point a camera at me and I'm right at home. So I'm hamming it up, telling them this story about how our Liberal government in Ottawa developed a plan to get rid of these zebra mussels. They cross-bred a northern pike with a piranha and created this exotic fish that chews the zebra mussels off the bottom of ships. They started to raise these fish in big open-water pens in Great Slave Lake, but one autumn they didn't get the pens out of the lake in good enough time and a big storm came along and broke open the pens and all these creatures escaped. They like eating zebra mussels, which is a good thing, but when there's no zebra mussels they have to eat something else. And it turns out that they love to eat aluminum. I told the Japanese film crew that one of the biggest dangers on Great Slave Lake is running into a school of these things when you're out in an aluminum fishing boat, because they'll go into a frenzy and starting eating your boat right out from under you.

I was about three-quarters of the way through this story when the other truckers started snickering. The gal who was working at the dispatch desk slapped her hand over her mouth and ran out of the room. And the Japanese director must have realized that I was having fun with him, because he told the guy to turn the camera off, and I never quite managed to finish telling the folks in Japan about this terrible threat to public safety created by Canada's Liberal government and their genetically modified predatory fish.

Anyway, these Los Angeles filmmakers came to Yellowknife looking for some characters to put in their show. They asked around Yellowknife, asking if there were any real characters they should meet, and just about everybody they met said, "You have to talk to Alex Debogorski."

I guess I've been around Yellowknife long enough that I'm a "local character." I'm loud, and some people think I'm funny. I know how to tell a pretty good yarn, and I tend to do things a little differently than everyone else. For example, when I ran for the office of mayor of Yellowknife, I used old car hoods and doors from my junkyard for election signs. I've been a bouncer, a coal miner, a union organizer, and a lay minister doing volunteer work in prisons. I have had eleven kids, all by the same wife. I've been married thirty-eight years (that's forty-five with the wind chill), and I don't watch television because it's not good for you. I write controversial columns about politics in the local newspaper and there's nothing I enjoy more than driving around Yellowknife a few hours after one of my columns comes out in the paper and seeing that people are all pissed off.

That's what I like—everybody up on their feet and yelling at one another. It's democracy in action. I guess that's what TV likes, right? They like people with loud mouths and strong opinions, so these TV people from Hollywood were out looking for this Debogorski guy, but I was in the middle of a panic trying to get heavy equipment out to a diamond exploration property I was looking after. It was located on Great Slave Lake, the three-hundred-mile-long lake that Yellowknife is located on. My buddy Dave Smith has this big barge, and we were trying to haul this heavy equipment out to their mining property at the other end of the lake. Most people quit going out on the lake at the end of September since it's too stormy and too dangerous after that. But this was October 25 and we had to deliver this stuff. There was no choice. It needed to be done. We made the delivery and a big storm came up on the way back. Waves crashed over our steel-hulled boat and we had the barge on a tow line. Ice formed on our decks. We finally had to turn around, finding shelter in Moose Bay, and there we bobbed up and down for five days.

I like reading. That's my favorite thing, but I hadn't brought any books. It was a work trip. All we had to pass the time was a DVD collection of *The Beverly Hillbillies*. So day after day, while the TV crew was waiting for us in Yellowknife, we had nothing to do but try and stay warm and watch these corny old reruns. I bet I could tell you everything you ever wanted to know about Jed Clampett.

Dawn Fitzgerald

We kept calling Louise to see if she had heard anything from Alex. She would just laugh, "No, he'll be home when he gets home."

Finally the boat arrived back in Yellowknife. It was about eleven o'clock at night, and we pulled down into the harbor with the headlights of our vehicle pointing at the boat. I don't think he knew we had been waiting for him, but that didn't throw him off. For the first twenty minutes we couldn't get a word in edgewise.

He succeeded in shocking or insulting everyone in the crew and anyone else who was standing around. You could see that he enjoyed offending people. I think of Alex as the original shock jock. It's quite hilarious, if you don't happen to be the person he's insulting. I remember saying to one of the crew, "I think we have a television show on our hands."

A Camera Followed Me Everywhere

They asked me if I wanted to consider being on the television show. I thought, *Well, my grandfather died before I was born and no one remembers what he looked like. I have all these children and eight grandchildren, and if this show succeeds, they can all watch me on television after I'm dead.*

Of course, there were no guarantees they were going to use me. The TV crew said they needed to film an interview and take it back to Hollywood and show it to their bosses.

We went to my friend Garth's wrecking yard. The only room we could find was on top of a thirty-five-foot flatbed trailer in his shop. So they set up their lights and cameras and prepared to film me. I remembered the time I was at the Klondike Festival down in Edmonton, entertaining those reporters with rude stories. That's when I learned that there's no point in pretending to be something you're not. So I just let 'er rip and gave them a piece of my mind. I had fun. I teased the pants off of all of them, especially this good-looking blonde named Dawn Fitzgerald who was in charge.

They took the film and went back to Hollywood. Well, to make a long story short, the bosses liked what they saw and they told me I had the job. So there I was, all of a sudden, a TV character. It was about the last thing on earth I ever expected would happen to me—a guy who lives about as far as you can go on this continent from Hollywood and doesn't even own a television. The makers of the show, Original Productions, said they were going to call it *Ice Road Truckers*, and they wanted to film us doing our day-to-day work. So I did my regular job loading, driving, and unloading my truck and they filmed all of it. They put cameras in the truck, one pointing at me and one pointing at the road. Occasionally a camera person would ride with me. Once in a while the camera people would get in the way and we would have a tiff. A bit of yelling, they would mend their ways, and we would be off again.

Having cameras in the truck and a camera crew following me turned out to be a lot of work. First, I lost my privacy. As a truck driver I enjoy my own company immensely. I am the funniest guy I know and the discussions I have with myself are both entertaining and mentally challenging, plus I rarely argue. With cameras present I often find myself wishing for some time alone.

Next, I am responsible for a cameraman in the passenger seat. He often asks dumb questions at the most inopportune moments. Sometimes there is a chase vehicle with cameras, so I have to make sure it doesn't get underfoot. Of course, the helicopter is a little distracting, too. Quite often in my off hours they want to film me sitting in a chair, talking. This cuts into my time kissing my wife.

Having run for political office, presented speeches in the city council, and worked as a union rep I was kind of accustomed to being in the public eye, and having been a breast-fed baby who was taken off the boob too soon predisposes me to liking attention! So I didn't mind being on camera. Of course, there are hundreds of hours of film taken during the typical ice road trucking season, so I always wonder what part of all these hours is going to be on the show, considering that eleven episodes only need less than eleven hours. Am I going to look like a hero, or am I going to look like an ass? They film so much that they can make me look either way. Oh, well. I usually end up looking a little bit like a hero and a little bit like an ass. I guess that's why they call it reality television!

The Cast of *Ice Road Truckers*

During the first year of the show, the film crew showed up and started filming us and establishing the main characters— guys like Drew Sherwood. Drew is not dangerous, but he can invent some interesting problems. He got his job driving with Hugh Rowland's team after answering an ad in a newspaper. Drew had experience highway driving, but no experience ice road trucking. Right off the bat, Drew was of the opinion that he would have no trouble adjusting to the ice road. His famous comment was, "I have no intention of going into a ditch, bro." Hugh considered Drew an arrogant rookie, and that was the tension between them. Of course, Drew ended up with all kinds of problems—a flat tire, a malfunctioning onboard computer—and Lee Parkinson, Hugh's mechanic, felt that

Drew had caused many of these problems himself. It all gave Drew a lesson in humility. Then he ended up going in the ditch, quitting the ice road, and going home.

We also met Rick Yemm, who, unlike Drew, can be downright dangerous without working at it. It comes to him naturally! He likes to push his equipment hard, and he is notoriously hard on his trucks. I think Hugh Rowland might have trained him. If you looked under the throttle pedal in Hugh's truck I bet you would find the floor dented from him pressing his foot down!

It's hard for me to comment on T. J. Tilcox because he was around for only one season. He was definitely very new in the ice road environment and had a rather wide-eyed, amazed approach to it all. And he didn't do too badly if you overlook a bashed fender, bruised ribs, and the fact he wasn't paid all his wages.

I felt sorry for poor Todd White, the long-haired, guitar-playing driver who got fired for speeding at the beginning of season one. He just didn't have it together and couldn't seem to get it together. Maybe some meditation and a lemon juice fast would fix him up.

Rick Fitch, the Tli Cho truck push in season one, was a big help to all of us. He got us our loads, gave us advice, patted us on the bum when we would get frustrated, and generally did a heck of a job getting us out of the yard and down the road. What he did was very important because if we didn't get a quick turnaround we could lose a pisspot full of money in a short two-month season. He turned us around fast, listened to all our BS, and put us in a better mood. They should have given him a medal.

And who can forget baby-face Jay Westgard? He always worked his butt off—like his dad and Uncle Dwayne—and was always available to help another driver out.

One trip I had to haul a load of fuel on a forty-five-foot flat deck. It was made up of forty-five-gallon drums stacked three high. I would have to go to the fuel bulk plant and they would bring them to the truck with a forklift. I would have to roll, stand up, and place each drum. They are close to 450 pounds each. Pallets are then put over all of them, and another layer of drums is placed on the pallets. This is really hard work, takes all afternoon, and I was sicker than a dog. I had a headache and was pooping my pants. Hell or high water, I was going to get the job done. I didn't want to miss a trip. I figured if I just kept putting one foot in front of another, whatever sickness I had would go away, but I was dying.

Dwayne Westgard happened to stop by. "How are things going, Alex?" And I answered, "The shits, and I am not feeling very well." Dwayne says, "Are you serious?" I say, "I sure am." Dwayne tells me to "Go home and lay down, I will load this and tie it down and call you when it's ready to go. It's going to take a while."

Sure enough, five hours later he calls me. I jumped out of bed and down the road I went. I felt a hundred times better than when I laid down. You know, I never gave Dwayne anything for helping me and I can't say we are really friends. But that is the kind of stuff that drivers do once in a while that makes the world a better place.

Season one was pretty popular, and we got the green light for another season of shooting, which took me to Inuvik, Northwest Territories, located on the Mackenzie River delta as it flows into the Arctic Ocean. We lost Jay, T. J., Lee, and Rick Fitch as characters, but we met a whole lot of new people. We got Eric Dufresne, who felt "convertible" at forty below in a blue jean jacket, his French accent shining through. Bear Swensen and his friend Charlie helped me immensely. They made sure I knew every nook and cranny of the Peterbilt winch truck that I was driving. They were low-key and made excellent friends. Thanks to those two, I had no problem with any of the winch work I did that winter.

Shaun Lundrigan, the Gruben's mechanic, never got excited and kept my truck running like a top. When I watched the show I was surprised to see that Rick Yemm got under his hide. It seemed to me that it would take a lot to make that man angry, so I guess Rick had what it took.

Rick and I generally worked for Gruben's transport and it was a good outfit. The equipment was definitely not new, but it all worked well for me. That Peterbilt I drove was a '95, but it pulled its heart out and never sputtered once. I passed a couple of new trucks sitting on the side of the road. We did our jobs, got paid well, and the superintendent, bosses, and owners left us alone.

I know Hugh "The Polar Bear" Rowland was tickled pink with Kirk and his company, Northwinds. He said the company and the owner were great.

Then there was Jerry Dusdal, the truck push from Mullen Transport. I am sure he and Rick Fitch from the first season of *Ice Road Truckers* had the same parents. He was excellent, always there to help, get us a load, baby us along, and always with a stupid grin. I guess he was a little bit funnier than Rick Fitch.

Season three brought Hugh and me to Alaska. Over the years I had heard about the Dalton Highway, Alyeska Pipeline, and the North Slope, but I never really thought I'd be blessed to work there. It took some time to get the American government to let us up there to work. Just in time we got our visas and the show went on.

I operated a truck simulator and took a number of road tests. I almost panicked. I really did get my license out of a popcorn box about thirty-five years ago and never had a road test. Here in Alaska I had numerous road tests and had to drive with different trainers for thousands of miles. I was thinking, *What if I really don't know how to drive? Do I use the clutch or not?*

The various trainers said, "Don't worry about it, and drive like you usually do. We've watched the first two seasons of *Ice Road Truckers* and think there's a very good chance you know how to drive."

Tony Molesky and Phil Kromm took "The Polar Bear" and me on our first trip up to Prudhoe Bay and back. Carlile, the company we worked for, teamed us up with experienced drivers who had similar driving styles. I got Jack McCahan, who was an absolute riot. There's probably nobody funnier and more politically incorrect in Alaska than Jack. If he goes down to the southern forty-eight I'm worried someone will shoot him. He's the guy in season three who said "Rookie Shit" and left as I was chaining up for Atigan. Heck, I'd never hold that against him.

Then I got my good buddy George Spears. I had to watch my rearview mirrors really closely because even the ground-hogs were passing me. You couldn't ask for a better man. After Vietnam he needed a job that would give him that occasional adrenaline rush. The Dalton Highway was it. So, thirty to forty years later, there he was with me following him. At the end of the season he retired back to his home in Illinois. I visited him there. He lives in the house where his grandparents raised him. He has a sister next door and spends time with his mum almost every day. She is in the old folks' home and isn't doing very well. He is happy and in his spare time he hauls corn for his neighbor.

Lisa Kelly drives a Kenworth Conventional. I think the smokestack is bigger round than she is, and heightwise she can just see over a 1100–24.5 tire. She is small, cute, and that big truck and her go round and round. Some of the guys get grumpy with her—especially behind her back. She has been threatened and some guys have said dirty stuff to her on the radio. But most drivers support her and are happy to see her. Being a woman in a man's world is a hard job.

Ron Dubbs, truck-driving man, traveled a couple of trips with me. He had to wait for parts to patch up his truck on one trip. He can actually sing. Well, almost. He would break into song on the CB radio once in a while. His singing wasn't good enough to make the show, I guess.

Little Tim Freeman (his dad is "Big Tim") traveled under George Spears's wing for his baptism up the Dalton. He and I had a minor run-in at the pub one night. Hugh and I had a beer and a burger there just before we all went home. Tim was also there. It turned out that after the camera guys stopped filming we decided to have a few too many double tequilas. While I was playing pool, Tim said something really crude to me and I cracked him in the jaw. It felt good. I could not remember the last time I dented my knuckles. I called Tim next day to apologize and he said, "No problem. It happens all the time when I am drinking. I take a little and I give a little."

Lane Keator is Carlile's terminal manager in Fairbanks. Everything we did went through him. He was a good guy to work for, treated me well, and occasionally was funny, but not as funny as the dispatcher, Tim Rickards. Tim's the guy who made sure that both our eyes were open and gave us a load. He was usually fair.

Jack Jessee has been on the Dalton a while but is a little uptight. The first year there I had little contact with him. The second year he presented himself as a father figure to me. I think he meant well. I asked him how old he was. He said he was thirty-eight. I thought, *That's my daughter Shielo's age. I now have a dad the same age as my daughter.*

Season four in Alaska put Ray Vellieux and Greg Boadwine in the show. Greg loves to talk. I think he wears out two sets of CB antennae per year because he is always broadcasting. I think he needs to work on the quality and cut back on the quantity when it comes to being an on-air comedian.

When I met Ray he felt I insulted him. I am not sure what I said. But most of the season he felt I was a bona fide ass and treated me as such. As God and luck would have it, he augered his truck in the snowbank. I came along and offered to help. I am sure he thought, *Oh, yeah, that will be a good photo opportunity to make Alex look good for the show and me look like an idiot.*

I shoveled for three and a half hours. I was soaking wet under my jacket. That was the hardest I worked in years. Digging Ray out of the ditch was the best example of teamwork. We had five Carlile drivers and three shovels. I have never seen five happier guys working in my life. The shovels were never idle. When I got tired I laid it down and someone else would pick it up. It was 25 degrees below zero and a sunny day. Ray had picked an excellent spot to hit the ditch. We dug the truck and trailer out and then chained up the drive axles of two loaded trucks. We attached two lengths of three-eighths chain and it all came out slick as a whistle. I hope Carlile paid all the fellows three and a half hours' pay because we saved the company a hefty tow bill. We were at the top of the ice cut pretty well in the middle of the North Slope of Alaska.

As truckers we compete for jobs and the few tasty scraps the dispatcher may throw our way. It may be a light load or it may be a backhaul. There is always some element of competition. Usually it is low-key until a guy like me runs into a fellow like Hugh Rowland. On the one hand, we get along and drink the odd beer or bottle of wine together. We have shared stories and spent hours visiting. On the other hand, he rubs me like sandpaper and turpentine. It is a paradox. I ignore him but at the same time try to keep close track of him so he doesn't pull one over on me. It's been this way for years.

Years ago I made a trip north on the ice road with Hugh and this fellow named Reg, who owns a Western Star truck and has been trucking on ice roads forever. On this particular trip he had said he hadn't been in a snowbank for longer than he can remember. It was a hard trip. We loaded and off we went again. We were tired. I pulled High out of the snowbank twice. I pulled Reg out twice. On the way back, as fortune would have it, I left Hugh behind when we stopped to sleep. Next trip he was twenty minutes behind. I hit the snowbank. My traveling partner pulled me out. It wasn't soon enough. Hugh caught up and realized the situation. For the next hour he is on the big radio. "Security, you should check this driver. He's having problems. A nurse should check him out. I don't think he's well!" I got to Lockhart, and the nurse asked me if I was okay. I told her I was fine but I thought the handicapped bear needed a psychiatrist! I think he is still pissed that I left him in the snow dust.

I am always leery about someone touching my truck. I take it as a personal affront when someone plays with my truck. Every time I get in my truck I try to check my air line hookup, make sure the fifth wheel hasn't been pulled and my fuel caps are tight, and that nothing goofy has been hung off the back. I do this in addition to the normal local check. I have had my air lines reversed, fuel caps come off, and found something dumb like a broken delineator stack on the back of the trailer. I have enough trouble keeping my crate going down the road without someone else actually causing me problems.

Not All the Good Trips End Up on TV

During season two of *Ice Road Truckers*, my most challenging trip was not filmed. It lasted about ten days. I traveled with a driver from Edmonton, Alberta, called Diesel. One could see the miles in the creases around his eyes. He had a mop of gray hair to his shoulders and a beard that a family of mice probably lived in.

We started out on February 28, 2008, at Atkinson Point, a Cold War American/Canadian radar site, which we were cleaning up. The trucks were reloaded on the ice at Tuktoyaktuk. We had two twenty-foot sea cans each, filled with contaminated soil, which we were taking to Swan Hills in Alberta. There the plant would make this stuff environmentally friendly.

Diesel would lead and guide me, since I truck mostly in the bush and not through "civilization." We go to Inuvik. The temperature is 42 below zero Celsius. I had trouble making the hill in town, going to the tire shop. Our shop thought I was having a fuel problem and gave me some additive. As we left Inuvik, to go south down the Dempster Highway to Whitehorse, in the Yukon Territory, we rolled through the closed weight scale. I couldn't figure out where the weights would be on the scale window, so I didn't know my axle weights.

As sometimes happens, even though I didn't know the trail, I ended up in the lead. We made it to Fort McPherson, where we crossed over the Mackenzie River on the ice. On we drove and we crossed the frozen Peel River. My problems started on the Peel River south hill, on which I spun out. Fortunately I was on my side of the road and Diesel had enough room to roar by. Otherwise I would have spun him out, too. In that case I would have gotten a reaming.

I put chains on all four drives and got going. I wore the jewelry all the way to Eagle Plains. Still, I had some trouble on the bigger hills. The truck seemed underpowered and had a problem with traction.

Traveling in the daylight, we covered some fine-looking country. Much of this area, south of Eagle Plains, was never covered with glaciers. It is prehistoric in every way. There are huge, rounded hills bordering large, rolling valleys. I could picture mammoths and saber-toothed cats. Biologists find plants and insects from pre–Ice Age times here. There is a butterfly species in which the female flies and the male walks (does this sound familiar?). The bones of mammoths and other Ice Age creatures are found in the permafrost by miners. There is still untold wealth in gold and other minerals back there, guarded by the bones of the prospectors who died looking for it.

We arrived at Klondike Corner, Yukon Territory, at one in the morning. After some sleep, we continued on to Whitehorse and arrived there late the next afternoon. I crossed the scale with an air leak and 17,000 pounds overweight on the three trailer axles. I was parked. The next day, Sunday, a crane came out and a light sea can on Diesel's truck was switched for my heavy one. My load became legal and now it was a lot easier for me to keep up. Diesel stopped giving me a hard time about my driving abilities, and the company I drove for got a ticket in the mail.

On March 5 we arrive in Swan Hills, Alberta. So far we've come across one tanker in the ditch near Fort St. John and one collision at Taylor Flats, in which a log truck missed a shift on a hill and almost stopped me. And I got cut off by a four-wheeler at least three different times. Now at Swan Hills, Diesel unloaded both trailers by sucking our four sea cans off with his winch truck. We then proceeded to Devon, just outside of Edmonton. There we waited a couple of days for loads to go back to Tuktoyaktuk, on the Arctic Ocean.

After having my truck gone over in the company shop in Devon, I got a load of lumber and headed north. The trip north was not quite as eventful as going south. A couple of hills on the Dempster put me and the truck to the test. There's one hill called "Shit House" that you climb in steps of 7 percent grades. The old Peterbilt would spin and I'd slack off. I'd step on it and the CAT engine would pick up the slack. This happened a number of times. I was actually surprised that I never once had to chain up.

The trip took me through the Northwest Territories, Yukon Territory, part of British Columbia, part of Alberta, and back again. I saw a lot of great scenery, from the Arctic Ocean to mountains, lakes, and farmland. We went from forty below in the North to ten degrees over zero in the South. We got everything from northern lights to streetlights. We had driven more than four thousand miles. It was a great trip with lots of adventure, but it never ended up on TV.

Fame and Fortune—Well, Fame, Anyway . . .

We've completed four seasons of *Ice Road Truckers*, and the show has actually gotten to be way bigger than even the producers hoped it would be. *Ice Road Truckers* has 3.5 million viewers in the United States and another 3.5 million viewers in Britain, give or take a few hundred thousand, and there are millions of other viewers in at least twenty-two other countries around the world. I don't really get involved in that part of the show, so I'm just throwing out rough numbers. What impresses me is not so much the size of the audience, which actually doesn't mean that much to me one way or another, but the stories that I hear from people—stories that show you how this show has really touched a nerve with people around the world.

A Mounted Police buddy of mine went down to Manila, the Philippines. He was driving down the highway from the airport, heaving this great sigh of relief that he was gonna see absolutely no one he knew for the next couple of weeks. And suddenly there I was, on this eighty-foot billboard, looking down at him. He said, "Is there nowhere I can go in this world to escape you, Debogorski?"

Another group of people from Yellowknife went on a wine tour of southern France. Apparently they went into this fancy vineyard to have a lunch and all the sophisticated French people were sitting around watching *Ice Road Truckers* on television. Richard Cadieux, an aboriginal buddy of mine, calls it "Creeping Debogorskism." He says, "Now that you're a television star there's gonna be no shutting you up." It's kind of odd being famous all of a sudden. Millions of people know who I am, but I don't know them. *People* magazine decided I'm one of "the sexiest men alive." (Louise always knew that.) If I pull up to a gas station in Chicago or Salt Lake City or Calgary, all I have to do is walk in to pay my bill and somebody will come up and slap me on the back. "Hey, Alex, how are you doing?"

I'm still in the habit of thinking, *Hey, this must be an old friend of mine!* So I'm standing there looking at his face, trying to figure out where I've met him before, and he'll say, "You don't know me, but I always watch your show!"

The funny thing is, they know more about the show than I do, because I don't watch television. I don't even allow one in the house. I guess the TV producers are going to want to kill me for saying this, but I think television is bad for you. I don't even watch movies. They're full of crime and ugliness, people scheming and lying and committing adultery and shooting each other. TV gives me a bad feeling about life. When you come from Eastern Europe, a land soaked in centuries of blood, there's nothing entertaining about watching people indulge their lower instincts. It's a short walk from civilization to savagery, and some people may enjoy watching it but I don't.

When I'm on the road, which is a lot of the time, the family will sometimes sneak a TV into the house. I can imagine them scrambling around upstairs when I arrive. "He's home! Hide the television!"

But they can't fool me. I'm like that giant in the fairy tale. *"Fee, fi, fo, fum, I smell the blood of a television!"*

I'll hunt for that television until I find it in a closet or under a bed, then I'll walk out onto the balcony and chuck it over the railing. There's no sound I enjoy more than a television exploding as it hits the driveway. So Alex Debogorski as a TV star, that's a joke for you.

I get to travel a lot in the off-season. I go to truck shows all over the United States, and there is always a big lineup of people who want to meet Alex the ice road trucker. Sometimes I'll take off and wander through the crowd, kissing hands and shaking babies. I will tickle people just to make them laugh. Nobody tickles strangers anymore. I guess it's considered politically incorrect. I'll tickle anybody—kids, women, old folks. I will tickle them and say, "There, that's your Alex Debogorski stimulus package."

One time I was at a truck show and there was the biggest, meanest-looking truck driver you ever saw. He was about 275 pounds, with black whiskers and busted-up knuckles and a scowl that would frighten a grizzly bear. Well, I sneaked up from behind and tickled him in the short ribs and he burst out laughing like a little kid.

I bet he hadn't laughed like that in forty years.

I do a fair amount of laughing myself. In fact, I've got this loud laugh that's kind of distinctive. Some people have even downloaded it as a ring tone on their cell phones. In any coffee shop in any city I will sometimes go unrecognized until I laugh. Then you see heads pop up over the restaurant, people looking around the room with these startled looks on their faces—*Hey, wait a minute! That sounds like Alex the ice road trucker!* Then they come up to me and shake my hand and tell me how much they enjoy the television show. Sometimes I barely have time to eat my lunch because I'm too busy talking to people. I don't mind it. In fact, it's enjoyable meeting all kinds of folks from different walks of life. Whether it's the kid who works at a gas pump or some famous star like Merle Haggard (he's a great guy, by the way), I try to speak to everyone man-to-man. Millions of people know me, but I have never met them. I get phone calls, letters, and presents. People call me for jobs. I travel to shows, sign autographs, sell T-shirts, visit and call sick people. I can make thousands of people's days just by showing up, calling, signing a picture, or just spending a few minutes with them. I guess the good Lord decided that Alex being a movie star at thirty would cause too much damage, so I'll be one at sixty instead.

I get to see a lot of new country, too, and I've driven all over the United States. I work on different equipment, with different people, in different countries. Now it looks like they're going to send us to India, to do some extreme trucking over there. That should be an eye-opener, a bunch of guys from the North of Canada, accustomed to working in 40 degrees below zero, working in places where it hits 113 above. Everybody in the family is all excited that Daddy is going to this exotic land.

But to tell you the truth, it's not a big thing to me. I've never gotten all worked up over seeing different places. People are what interest me. People and ideas. All the places I want to visit are in my head. If I'm in a new place I'm happy just going to visit a junkyard. Most people like to visit beaches and mountains and exotic resorts. That's fine; they can have their pretty scenery. Give me a junkyard anytime. I'll take a stroll though a wrecking yard, and that makes me happy. The place is real and so are the people.

I enjoy working on the show and I like the people on the crew. Mind you, they've got a slightly different attitude than we do. People in television are always hoping something bad will happen. If it's a hockey game, they're hoping a fight will break out. If it's a car race, they're hoping there's going to be a big smashup. On the ice roads, the TV crew is always hoping a truck is going to spin out or fall off a mountain or something. That gets them all excited. We're hoping for just the opposite. We're always hoping that absolutely nothing is going to happen today. And of course if something does happen, they're always aiming that camera at your face, hoping that you're going to show some kind of emotion. Is Alex furious? Has this darned ice road finally pushed him to the breaking point? I try to act like I'm sedated on lithium so they won't be concentrating on me. No matter what happens, I don't react. "Hmm, my wheels just fell off and I'm heading for a cliff. Well, that's interesting . . ."

The folks I meet when I'm traveling the world assume that I have made a lot of money from the TV show. Well, I guess the show has made some people wealthy, but I'm not one of them. Being the star of a reality television show doesn't earn you a lot of money. I've been working hard all my life and I'll work hard until the day I die. That's just the way it is.

But if you ask me, "Are you rich?" I'll say, "Yes, I'm rich."

I'm rich in the things that matter. I have a beautiful, loving wife and a great big tribe of kids and grandkids.

No matter how you slice it, I think it is fair to say I've come a long ways from that summer night when I was just a lonely kid sitting on the banks of the river, wondering what the heck I was going to do with my life. I'd like to take credit for making it to the big time. I'd like to say that I knew it all along—that sooner or later people would notice my handsome face and brilliant intellect—but it's all just a chain of lucky breaks. Sure, I'm a hard worker, and yes, I think God helps you out if you ask for it, but God has more important things to do than manage my show-business career. And there are lots of good, hard-working truck drivers out there who don't end up on eighty-foot-high billboards.

I think the show is such a big success because people are regaining their admiration for the blue-collar workers—the men and women who go out there every day and bust their asses trying to make society work. At one time, wealthy people got respect just because they were rich. We figured, they must be pretty incredible people, or else how did they earn all that money? I've kind of noticed that attitude has died off in the past ten years or so. The average person is not necessarily fascinated by the rich and famous. You've had all these stories in the news about crooked investment dealers and fat-cat bankers and corporate executives flying around in private jets and getting sweetheart severance packages while their employees get laid off and the company goes down the tubes. So the average person doesn't necessarily respect the big-shot politician or the millionaire anymore. We've seen too many of these characters get caught stealing money or sneaking around with young girls or lying to the TV cameras with big smiles on their faces. The only difference between them and a skunk is the two-hundred-dollar haircut.

I remember when those terrorists flew those planes into the Twin Towers. It wasn't a bunch of millionaires who came running to help those people trapped inside. It was the average Joe, the firefighters, the medics, the beat cops. They took one look at those buildings and they knew there was a good chance their jobs were going to cost them their lives that morning. Guys were calling their wives to say goodbye as they went inside. The point is, they went in anyway. They weren't doing their jobs to get rich. They were going inside because somebody had to do it.

And later on, when the smoke cleared, it was the construction guys and the iron workers who showed up to take apart the wreckage. Nobody asked them to show up. They just grabbed their hard hats and laced on their boots and went down there to pitch in. They weren't even getting paid. I think that's when America remembered that its hero has always been the workingman.

The working guy gets up every morning and makes this world function. He might be unplugging your sewer or fixing a power line high up on a pole or driving a farm tractor, but you'd be in a lot of trouble without him. I'm proud of being a member of the working class, and I'm glad I've spent most of my life behind the wheel. I like the feeling of being out on the open road, being my own boss, and getting the job done. I hope I die with my wheels spinning.

CREDITS

Quotes by John Denison (page 152), Jim Chapman (pages 164–165), and Adele Boucher (page 176) are from *Trucking North: On Canada's MacKenzie Highway* by Roberta Hursey, published in 2000 by Detselig Enterprises, Ltd. Reprinted by permission.

Photo credits: Insert page 6 top: Lynn Fowler; insert page 8 top: Ron Dickson; insert page 8 bottom, left and right: Wayne Gzowski.

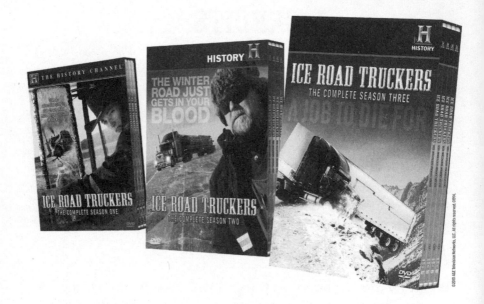